Maternity Rolls

Pregnancy, Childbirth and Disability

Heather Kuttai

Fernwood Publishing · Halifax and Winnipeg

Editing: Christy Ann Conlin
Design: Brenda Conroy
Cover design: John van der Woude
Printed and bound in Canada by Hignell Book Printing

Mixed Sources
Product group from well-managed
forests and other controlled sources
www.fsc.org Cert no. SW-COC-003438
© 1996 Forest Stewardship Council

Published in Canada by Fernwood Publishing
32 Oceanvista Lane
Black Point, Nova Scotia, B0J 1B0
and #8 - 222 Osborne Street, Winnipeg, Manitoba, R3L 1Z3
www.fernwoodpublishing.ca

Fernwood Publishing Company Limited gratefully acknowledges the financial support of the Government of Canada through the Canada Book Fund, the Canada Council for the Arts, the Nova Scotia Department of Tourism and Culture and the Province of Manitoba, through the Book Publishing Tax Credit, for our publishing program.

Library and Archives Canada Cataloguing in Publication

Kuttai, Heather, 1969-
Maternity rolls: pregnancy, childbirth and disability / Heather Kuttai.

ISBN 978-1-55266-342-4

1. Kuttai, Heather, 1969-. 2. Pregnancy in women with disabilities. 3. Women with disabilities — Canada — Biography. 4. Paraplegics — Canada — Biography. 5. Parents with disabilities — Canada — Biography. 6. Athletes with disabilities — Canada — Biography. I. Title.

RC406.P3K87 2010   362.4'3092   C2010-900020-X

Contents

To Patrick and Chelsea
for giving me a story to tell

and for Darrell
because this is his story too
143

Acknowledgements

I would like to thank my supervisor, Dr. Donna Goodwin, for her tremendous support and unrelenting faith in this project. I would have given up many times if it had not been for her ability to say all the right things at just the right times.

I would like to acknowledge my committee members, Dr. Kent Kowalski and Dr. Louise Humbert, who gave me their time, attention, feedback and good ideas. I also want to recognize SSHRC for the funding I received.

To Dr. Rodney LiPiShan, I give my deepest gratitude for listening to me during my second pregnancy and for trusting my words when no one else would.

To Dr. Roger Turnell, I offer my thanks and appreciation for guiding me through my first pregnancy with humour, confidence and an open mind. Thanks also to Dr. Silverton, who "found" Chelsea when she made her entrance to this world.

Thanks to my first coach, Finn Petersen, for teaching me how and why to have confidence in myself. I owe him a great debt.

My appreciation includes Dr. Vera Pezer, who continues to be a mentor to me long past our professional work together. She continues to teach me a great deal about leadership, being strong and doing the right thing, even and especially when it is most difficult to do just that. Those lessons helped me a lot during my writing.

I owe a debt to my parents-in-law, Lois and Raymond Seib, for their willingness and abilities to drop everything to help me and my family when we need them the most.

Thanks goes to my niece, Tanya Norman, for providing my daughter (and sometimes my son) with a second home and happy times when I needed to write my thesis and for going above the call of duty many times.

My gratitude extends to two good friends, Jacki Andre, who offered to read my first draft with an exceptional attention to detail, and Frank Kusch, who, during one of our many intense conversations over glasses of red wine, helped me come up with my book title. Thanks also to Dr. Lesley Biggs and Dr. Pamela Downe for their support, encouragement and faith in me.

Thank you, Sharon Haave, for the letters, light and love.

To CBC Radio for both keeping me company while I wrote and for providing quality music to creatively inspire me every day, thank you.

I would be remiss not to recognize the women with disabilities I have "met" through the literature they were brave enough to write. I found a community of women through their words. In particular, I want to recognize the late Audre Lorde, a self-named "Black warrior lesbian post-mastectomy feminist poet," who wrote: "For we have been socialized to respect fear more than our own needs for language and definition, and while we wait in silence for that final luxury of fearlessness, the weight of that silence will choke us" (1997, p. 22). It is this declaration that I kept posted above my computer and read every day to keep myself both motivated and grounded.

I want to express my love and profound appreciation for the sport of target shooting. The experiences I had with the shooting sport gave me invaluable opportunities to learn how to be a better person.

Thanks to the production people at Fernwood: Debbie Mathers, Beverley Rach and Brenda Conroy, for their hard work. Special thanks to Wayne Antony for believing in this project, and to Jessica Antony for the final copy edit of this book. I also give thanks to my editor and "kindred spirit," Christy Ann Conlin, whose challenging questions and brilliant instincts made this book better.

Acknowledgement and profound gratitude goes to my husband, Darrell Seib, who is the best possible person to accompany me through this life and through this writing journey. I know for certain that I could not have completed this project without him and it would be impossible to thank him in words for everything he does and all that he is. He also knows more about Microsoft Word than anyone I have ever met, which admittedly was very convenient.

Lastly, I want to acknowledge my good parents, George and Betty Kuttai, for expecting great things from me and for being positive, hopeful and unconditionally supportive. Without their profound perseverance and formidable strength during difficult times, life could have turned out very differently for me. At least in part, this story belongs to them, too.

Prologue

I am a forty-year-old white, heterosexual woman who is married, the mother of two children and lives in a house in a quiet, middle-class neighbourhood. In many ways, my life seems like the quintessential picture of a nuclear family living what is considered by many to be a traditional life.

However, my life is not as conventional as it appears, particularly because I am also a paraplegic and I use a wheelchair for mobility. My disability dramatically changes the picture of tradition. To help you understand why this is true, I need to tell you the story that starts with me, a little blond-haired farm girl, an accident that changed everything and how everything changed again when I grew up, became pregnant and had children of my own.

I have told a version of this story many times, during conversations with my son's teachers when I meet them at the beginning of each new school year, to strangers at cocktail parties, to each new doctor or medical professional from whom I seek medical advice, and to groups of people when I have performed a keynote speech at a conference or given a guest lecture. The main details are basically always the same, the length may vary and the level of disclosure inevitably varies depending on my comfort, level of trust, amount of courage I am feeling and emotional detachment from the story I am experiencing at the time. Much of this story has been captured on paper in my journals, some is filed away in hiding places in my own head. Some of the story exists in the song lyrics written by others that "speak to me," some is what I have heard my parents tell and some simply exists on my tongue. I have lived my life through, and I have been shaped by, this story. It needs and deserves to be written, read, seen, spoken and heard.

November 28, 2009

The candles are being lit on the birthday cake. Sixteen shiny little faces beam at my daughter, Chelsea, who is four years old today. Darrell is poised with his camera to capture the moment; Patrick, my twelve-year-old son, stands next to me with his hand on my shoulder, somehow sensing that I need the support. Someone turns out the lights and one small voice excitedly whispers, "This is the best part."

We start to sing "Happy Birthday." I do not even get as far as "dear Chelsea" when tears start and I cannot sing another word. I just let them fall and instead I mouth the words. Across the room, Darrell sees me and gives me a sympathetic smile. I cannot take my eyes off my little girl and I let myself embrace Patrick's loving energy. All at once I remember what it was like when my belly was ripe with their growth and what it was like to give birth to my babies and meet them for the first time. And I say to myself, "You are so lucky. Look at these beautiful children. Your children. This was never expected to happen. You, a mom. Imagine that."

1

Girl, Interrupted

The Accident

Tell me the story
'bout when you were young
Leave in the part
where the hero gets stung
(Annie Lennox, "Lost")

On a scorching afternoon on June 4, 1976, my mother gave me the choice between catching the school bus to go home to our farm after I was finished with my school day or waiting a few extra minutes for her to finish up her meeting with the Catholic Women's League that was happening across the street. Although I was only six years old I had enough experience riding the bus to know that the long ride home would be uncomfortable, sweaty and hot. I decided to wait for my mom. Besides, I did not want the older kids on the bus to tease me about what I was wearing like they had in the morning.

A few days earlier, a boy in my class told me that I was not like the other girls because I never wore dresses and that if I wanted to be pretty I had better start wearing some. So on this hot, sticky day, I wore a simple lavender gingham cotton dress and as I waited for Mom to pick me up and take me home, I was impressed and surprised with how much cooler a dress was than my usual blue jeans. Nevertheless as my mom, my older sister, Joanne, and my niece, Kirsten, and I drove home with all the windows rolled down in a wishful attempt to bring some relief the way only a cool breeze can on that kind of sweltering day, I lay down in the backseat of our car and imagined how good a cool lemonade would taste under the shade of our garden's crabapple tree.

My day dreams were interrupted by what I can only remember as a chaotic mix of images: my mother's head cut and bleeding; strangers talking in loud, urgent voices; the sound of my sister crying and feeling pain and discomfort from a sheet of cardboard behind my back and shoulders that someone had laid me on. I can still feel the asphalt underneath my fingers.

13

I could hear Joanne crying. My mom was frantically looking around for her lost earring; meanwhile with a strange calmness I realized I could not feel my legs. When I told my mom this, she explained to me that I was in shock. Although I do not know how my other family members learned about the accident, I remember my dad arriving on the scene, and how my brother Jim leaned over me to offer encouraging words.

The next thing I remember is a cold, brightly lit emergency room where I was again lying on my back and feeling extreme pain. When I overheard the doctor tell my mother that my dress would have to be cut off because he could not risk doing damage to my body while pulling it over my head, I screamed and cried. While I could not feel my legs, while I was experiencing excruciating pain in the places I could still feel, surrounded by strangers in a strange place and knowing instinctively that something was terribly wrong with me, my most prevailing thought was how I did not want that dress to be mutilated by a pair of scissors. I honestly remember thinking, "How will I ever be pretty again?" In my mind, that dress meant I was a girl. In that moment, the idea of losing that identity was somehow more tragic than what my body was experiencing.

Where's the Girl: Lowered Expectations

> *It's just your expectations*
> *should be lower*
> *(Edwyn Collins, "Low Expectations")*

Ironically, my grief over the dress's destruction was a foreshadowing for how my identity would also alter. As a girl with a spinal cord injury who uses a wheelchair, I experienced a markedly different set of developmental, social and biological expectations than non-disabled girls my age seemed to experience as they grew up. For example, it was assumed that I would always need someone to look after me; that I would not live independently; that I would not be able to attract a man, date, marry; and certainly not have a sexual relationship, have children, and be able to look after those children. Because my spinal cord was injured at a young age, I believe this expectation that I would live a socially and sexually barren life was even more poignant for me than for women who acquire their disabilities later in life. At age six, I had not yet, of course, developed sexually in either physical, social or emotional ways. I was just simply too young. Women who acquire their disabilities later in life may still struggle with their identities, but generally they have had more time and opportunities to develop their sexuality.

French philosopher Michel Foucault describes social forces, especially those associated with sexual identity, as strong influences on how we define who we are and how we present ourselves.[1] Feminist writer Judith Butler argues that there are societal expectations of men and women that are "accepted" ways to "perform" gender, such as women as nurturers.[2] While I think she is correct, I think that there is also a gendered experience of disability that assumes that to live with disability is to live without sexuality.[3] The asexual status that is often attributed to people with disabilities was, I believe, stronger for me than for other people who are injured after they have achieved their sexual identities, because, unlike people who experience spinal cord injuries later in life, I had no opportunity to develop an "adult" construction of sexuality or the pre-pubescent or adolescent constructions of sexuality. After a spinal cord injury, sexual identities and adult social roles are often denied.[4] When my spinal cord was injured, part of my identity as a girl was ruined too, just like the remnants of my lavender gingham dress.

Having my spinal cord injured and becoming a paraplegic so early in life, I did not have many chances to achieve much of a sexual identity and there were no expectations from most of the adults in my life, such as family members, teachers, friends and neighbours, that I ever would. There were none of the comments that my peers received, like, "Heather will be a heartbreaker" or "Heather will be a good mommy someday." Growing up with the unspoken yet prevailing attitudes that I would not live a fruitful and productive life, that I would not live independently from my parents, or become anyone's employee, girlfriend, wife or mother, became undeniably, consciously and subconsciously, ingrained in how I identified and saw myself. It was more acceptable and easier for me to see myself, and to be seen by others, as a "cute kid," which is a more androgynous and asexual label, than as a "pretty girl," which is decidedly more feminine and by consequence, sexual. I seemed to be surrounded by pretty classmates and cousins. I was always aware that wheelchairs were not pretty, and since I associated myself with my chair, I thought I could not be pretty either. My desires for feeling as though I were a pretty girl led into confusion about my feelings of sexuality as I entered my teenage years. If I was not pretty, then I could not be sexual, and if I was not sexual, then I was not a real woman, or a whole person.

This does not mean I did not try to be pretty. I styled my hair, I wore the fashions of the day and I used makeup. But I did this mostly with the intention of proving to everyone that I was a "real" girl. I ached for the validation. Throughout dating, my first sexual experiences and even marriage, I made steps towards realizing my own intrinsic worth as a sexual person, but in the end I did not realize how much I had internalized the notion that to live with a disability is to live without sexuality until I became pregnant for the first time. It was then that my sexuality could no longer be denied by anyone, not even me.

August 18, 1996

> I just don't know how to feel. I have to go to the bathroom a lot and every time I do, I expect to find the blood stains of my period, informing me that this whole thing has been a huge misunderstanding. It's not that I don't want this baby; I just can't believe it is happening. Could something this natural, this normal, really be happening to my body? My body that has never been my friend. The bottom line is this: I did not expect I was ever this female.

I remember yearning for my period when I was about twelve or thirteen, as I know many girls that age do. *Are you there, God? It's Me, Margaret*, the coming-of-age novel by Judy Blume whose main characters were obsessed with bras and first periods, was so popular among my classmates that it was impossible to sign out of our school's library. Desperate for this rite of passage, I think I felt the same way as the characters in that book and my friends did. As it happened, my period came in my mid-teens, and although this is perfectly normal, at the time I was sure the delay was because of my paralysis. My paralysis was responsible for everything. That notion, as irrational as it might seem to me now, stayed with me for years. So once I was married and Darrell and I knew we wanted a family, we did not know if my body was capable of getting and staying pregnant, or delivering a baby. As well, unlike our other married friends, no one ever asked us when or if we were going to start a family. The assumption was that we would not or could not get pregnant, so no one asked. We decided to try and get pregnant, but if I could not conceive (again, I thought if that was the case it would be because of my paralysis), we would adopt. So when I missed my period in August 1996, I did not think I could be pregnant. My friend, Pam, who is a nurse in my doctor's office, convinced me I needed a pregnancy test, and bet me a milkshake that it would be positive. Obviously, I lost that bet.

Home Girl

> *Saturated with negative images*
> *and a limited range of*
> *possibilities is strange*
> *(Shad, "Brother")*

In the early months after my injury, it was suggested by my then rehabilitation doctor and the rehabilitation centre's head nurse that I would be better off living and going to school at the Children's Rehabilitation Centre in Saskatoon (an hour and a half drive away from my home), at least for a while, lest, in their opinion, I become too much of a physical, emotional and financial burden on my parents. At the time, the construct of disability was primarily dictated by a "medical model" that saw disability as a pathological problem that resided in the "patient" and required the solutions of rehabilitation and medical intervention to correct his or her "deficiencies."[5] The scientific system that underlies the medical model has certainly brought about medications and other technologies that improve physical functioning for people with disabilities; however, many more difficulties for people with disabilities reside within the social contexts of disability.[6] This was definitely true for me and my parents. Whereas my parents and extended family wanted me back at home and found it relatively simple to add an outside lift to our house and renovate our bathroom to include grab bars, it was considerably more challenging to weave me back into the social systems of school and our community, where oppressive and negative stereotypes about disability were firmly ingrained. It was, for example, easy for me to make friends, especially with those who were curious about the wheelchair. But it was also difficult for me to retain those friends once my disability was noticed by other peers who chose to tease or make fun of me. I would quickly become someone who was a threat to my friend's social currency and I would be dropped. As I reflect on my childhood friendships, I realize that I certainly had some true friends who were loyal to me, but I did not feel secure in those friendships. Indeed, I was often afraid of being left alone. I wanted to belong, to fit in and to feel welcome.

There were times when I was consciously included in my community. My elementary school principal made sure that I was welcome back in my school. A ramp was constructed, my desk with the built-in seat was swapped for a table and the girl's bathroom was modified. But when my best girlfriend joined after school clubs in another part of town, and I was told I could not join because there were steps to get in, I was sad. When I attended her dance recitals and saw her in her beautifully embroidered Ukrainian dresses, I was delighted to watch her dance, but heartbroken because I thought I never would. It was not that I necessarily wanted to be a Ukrainian dancer like her; I just wanted to feel like I was a part of something too.

Watching your child struggle socially is difficult for any parent and mine were no exception. At the same time, they also were without real-life examples of other people like me and like themselves. In other words, not only was I without expectations and social norms, so were my parents, and therefore they were also without imagination for what the rest of my life would be like. Psychotherapist Rhoda Olkin argues that "there are so few role models... that parents often have no vision of what their children can become."[7] My paralysis and the uncharted territory of my new disability-related needs seemed to overshadow everything else that I was or could imagine becoming.

As I wrote this book, the following parts about my childhood and the stories of my parents (especially those of my mom), became intertwined. My mom was saddened after she read my manuscript the first time. There were things she read that I had never told her about before. It was never my intention to cause her pain and although I have not altered this manuscript or changed the stories, I want to make one thing clear: I love my mother. Although my mom was not perfect, and although there were things I wish she had done differently, who among us has not felt that about our parents? My children are still young, and yet I often lie awake at night and ask myself if I am doing a good job or if I am measuring up as a parent. I usually come to the conclusion that I am doing the best I can. While I cannot imagine how hard it was to raise me, what I know for certain is that my mom loves me and that she did her best. In fact, without anyone to turn to, without any sort of guide, she did much better than that. Both of my parents were strong and brave at times when it would have been easier to give up.

It's a Girl Thing: Longing for Long Hair

> *She never really expected more*
> *That's just not the way we are raised ...*
> *She's looking in the mirror*
> *She's fixing her hair*
> *(ani difranco, "Fixing Her Hair")*

In the fall that I returned to school after the accident, this time sitting in a wheelchair, wearing pants and sporting a pixie cut, I remember expressing to my parents that I wanted to grow my hair longer so that I could wear "pony tails like the other girls at school." My mom encouraged my short hair, explaining that short hair was easier and that I had "enough problems without having long hair to look after, too." I was hurt then, but I do not blame her for feeling this way now. I do not doubt that if she had known how much it meant to me she would have let me grow my hair, but I did not push the issue. I remember feeling the need to protect my mother from further sadness very early after the accident. I know that she also had strong feelings of protection towards me and that she was doing her best to care for me. It must have been intensely difficult for her to do all the things for me that she was required to. I think about this long hair dilemma that my mom must have faced every time I now wash my own daughter's hair and painfully have to comb through her tangles. Perhaps my mom was speaking to the exhaustion she faced being both my mother and my primary care-giver (she was, after all, responsible for all my physical needs at this point — from physical therapy, to lifting me in and out of bed, to transferring me in the bathroom and doing all my catheterizations), and combing through hair tangles was just one thing she could not add to her already long list of obligations. Or perhaps she was reluctant or even fearful to see me resemble a girl and all the complications that came with that (like boyfriends, dating) in addition to the identity of disabled, paraplegic and needing a wheelchair.

Parenting is an incredibly difficult job. I think it was even more difficult for my parents, especially my mom. It is difficult for her to talk about the accident and my childhood because she still bears personal responsibility for what happened. I do know that it was difficult for her to allow me to move through the rites of passage that other girls my age were experiencing. I am sure it is difficult for any mother to watch her daughter move from child to adolescent but, although I know she was doing her best, I think it was especially hard for mine. Without knowing what kind of a future existed for me, without any models or examples for her to look to for hope or inspiration, and with a deep sense of responsibility for my bodily care, I think my mom viewed me, at least at times, as weak, dependent and helpless. She once confessed to me that she used to lie in bed and wonder what I would ever do without her. Fair enough. She had to do so much for me. She also had no idea what my future would be like. The only people with disabilities she had ever really been exposed to were elderly or in need of constant care. These characteristics are how people with disabilities are often seen and they are the opposite of how a mature, sexual person is seen, which is typically as strong, self-reliant and physically competent.[8] As an adult, I often marvel at how difficult it must have been for my mom, and how strong she was.

It's a Girl Thing: My First Bra

When I was twelve or thirteen years old and aware that other girls were starting to wear bras, I expressed that I wanted to wear one too. In my mind, this garment was a significant mark of a "real" girl. My mom was reluctant to purchase one for me, telling me that I was "not ready." She was probably right — my body was likely not in need of one. However, afterward, I felt ashamed for asking and I did not mention it again. Instead, I frequently left the Sears catalogue open to the bra section on the end of my bed, as a hint and subtle reminder. When she finally gave in to my unspoken pleadings and bought me a bra, it was not made of the shiny, satiny and stretchy material that my cousins and friends were so proud of wearing. It was plain white cotton and I was disappointed. I wanted what I imagined everyone else had. I wanted a pretty bra because receiving it would have been recognition that I was a pretty girl who was growing up. I remember wearing the bra anyway and the first time I had it on at school, with the outline of those telltale straps showing through my t-shirt, certain that everyone noticed and was talking about it. I imagined they were surprised that I had one on and that they were thinking, "Heather is just like everyone else."

Foucaudian analyses state that social forces, especially those related to sexuality, have an intense influence on how individuals represent themselves. Foucault would also say, however, that when these forces are exerted, resistance to the power of those forces may also occur.[9] My desire for a pretty bra was much stronger than my sense of obedience towards my mother. In an act that resisted the power of my mother's act to provide me with the kind of undergarment that I thought exemplified prettiness and sexiness, I bought my own bra at the local Kresge's store with some saved birthday money. I chose it off the shelf and then hid the small box it came in between a paperback novel and a chocolate bar. My anxiety that someone would catch me and tell me that I was not allowed to buy it made my breath come in short gasps; however, once I paid for it and hid it in the shopping bag, I relaxed a little. I had no idea how I was going to keep it as a secret from my mother once it was home in my dresser drawer. The entire act was worth it once I arrived home and put on that bra, that bra that was just like the one that the other girls were wearing. While my mom was trying to exert control over what she thought I should wear, I was exerting a reciprocal power by demanding a part of my identity that I was desperate to claim. Perhaps I was also frustrated with how many times I missed out on the many social constructions that seemed to happen naturally for my female peers: I did not wear dresses, I did not wear my hair long and, although I attended all my junior and high school dances, I was not the girl that anyone ever had a crush on, I very rarely danced with a boy and I did not date. There were other more subtle markings of what it meant to be a girl — the way they moved, walked, stood, danced, and sat with their ankles crossed. The purchase of a bra was something I could control, although the act came with the threat of shame and anxiety. However, I had what I wanted and, at least in one small way, I felt like a "real" girl.

It's a Girl Thing: Dresses

> *If I don't want to, I don't have to*
> *I don't have to wear a dress*
> *I can sit with my legs apart*
> *(Betty Blowtorch, "Dresses")*

I chased my sense of feeling female for years; some days I think I still do. I still feel a twinge of displacement and a little bit of shame when I shop for lingerie. For me, symbols of femininity were tangible objects that were external to me and that made sense to a little girl: long hair, bras and dresses. After that precious lavender gingham dress was cut off of my small six-year-old body that day in the Emergency Room, I do not remember wearing a dress again for three years. By then, I was marking my ninth birthday at the Hospital for Sick Children in Toronto, where I was a patient.

I had arrived at the Hospital for Sick Children because my mom had read about the advancements that this hospital and its neurosurgeons were making towards spinal cord injuries research. She bravely picked up the telephone from her farm house kitchen in small town Saskatchewan and dialed one of the doctors in Toronto she had read about. Astonishingly, the doctor told her to book a flight and bring me to the hospital and he would take me on as a patient. One of the first things the medical staff did for me was remove the indwelling catheter with the leg bag that was strapped to my calf and subsequently taught me how to do independent, self-catheterizations, a process they promised me and my parents would add years to my life by ensuring fewer bacterial infections and less stress on not just my bladder but also my kidneys and overall blood stream. But from a nine-year-old's perspective, it also meant that the ugly, embarrassing and smelly leg bag would be gone and because my legs would be free and bare, I could wear a dress again. I was excited about this idea. Mom and Dad went out and bought me a dress for the birthday that I celebrated as a patient, and I remember the special event of unwrapping it in my hospital room at SickKids. Although I no longer have it (I wish I did), I can picture it vividly: it was buttery cream-coloured soft cotton with a lilac paisley trim. It even had a bow in the back. Dad admitted to me that no one would be able to see the bow when I was sitting in the wheelchair, but because both he and I knew it was there, that was good enough. I loved that dress. And I loved my parents for buying it for me and for somehow understanding that the dress could give me something I was missing: a sense of being ordinary, feminine, pretty and therefore, in my mind, valuable, beautiful and whole.

Dresses continued to be an important symbol of my female identity into my adolescent years. For example, I desperately wanted to wear a dress to my first junior high school prom. My mom seemed resistant, telling me that because I could not cross my legs nor keep my knees together while sitting in the wheelchair, that a dress was not the best option for me. There was an unspoken "girl" rule that to sit in a dress with your knees apart meant an increased potential for exposing something that best remained covered up. This risk of exposing of my private area, an area that is inherently sexual, only served to further confuse me. On one hand, I received the message that my disabled body rendered me an asexual being; on the other hand, I was also being told that the dress could expose that which made me sexual. Nevertheless I still wanted a dress. I know Mom sensed my disappointment and as she was a skilled seamstress, she offered to make me a "nice jumpsuit" out of whatever fabric I wanted. Eventually, however, I was either persistent or outwardly depressed enough that she gave in to my desire to look pretty and feminine and Mom sewed me a dress to my first prom, just like the other girls. Like the other significant dresses in my life so far, it was also a shade of lavender. It was also cut in the brazen style of the mid 1980s. It was made of taffeta, had a fitted top and huge puffy sleeves that were in the off-the-shoulder style of the day. Underneath the shiny taffeta skirt of the dress, I duct-taped my knees together and I felt like a princess. I went to the girl's bathroom midway through the dance. It was jammed with girls competing for mirror time, combing their hair, applying makeup and adjusting their dresses. I was so proud of my beautiful dress. I had received so many compliments on it and on how it looked on me. I was about to leave the hustle and bustle of the bathroom when a girl I knew quite well exclaimed that the back of my dress was so low that it showed my surgical scars. There was no mistaking the shock and mild disgust in her voice. Thunderstruck, my humiliation grew as the girls crowded around me, wanting to take a look at the scars that were peeking out from the back of the bodice.

The event was not the first time that I would be ashamed of my physically different body at school. Although many efforts were made to integrate me in the classroom with my non-disabled peers, once I was attending junior high, I did not take part in many of the physical activities that boys and girls my age were involved in, including the physical education programs. No attempts to modify a program were made for me. I was often required by the teacher to change out of my school clothes and wear a gym uniform as I watched my non-disabled peers from the sidelines during physical education class. I went to the locker room and changed into the gym shirt, along with everyone else, and then I would sit and watch the class. I dreaded entering that locker room; I felt ridiculous. Yet, it was a ritual that everyone else participated in, so I continued to do it without question. I do not remember anyone else ever questioning it either. I remember one time when a teacher had me try some free weights off in one corner of the gym while my classmates played volleyball. However, I was even more self-conscious then, like I was sticking out even more than sideline-sitting. In this half-hearted attempt to involve me, I also felt like an imposter, like someone who did not deserve to be there, which was inevitably worse than just watching.

Shooting Like a Girl

At the same time, however, our visit to the Sick Children's Hospital in Toronto opened my parent's eyes to the benefits of physical activity. The medical specialists there encouraged Mom and Dad to involve me in any kind of activity that would get my body moving. The benefits, we were told, would be better blood circulation and lower risk of heart disease and diabetes. They also felt it would improve my feelings of self-worth and lower my risk of depression. In particular, Mom and Dad were motivated to have me try swimming. Because the local swimming pool was not accessible in many ways, (I remember not being able to fit my wheelchair into the change rooms) and because my parents never did anything halfway, they researched, designed and built an indoor swimming pool right outside my bedroom door, and swimming became a daily activity for me.

At the same time, spending time outdoors, sport and physical activity were also integral parts of my family's life. Although I was an active little girl before the accident, with my girlhood interrupted, priorities for activity changed. Leisurely sunshiny playtime on the farm amongst the crabapple trees was replaced by a lot of time spent indoors and my childhood became complicated by bladder infection prevention, healing pressure sores, physiotherapy and regular doctors' appointments in the "big city" of Saskatoon. My family made conscious efforts to include me in the fun I had always been involved with before my injury. My parents and my brothers took me snowmobiling, sledding and even skating. My brothers Ernie and Jim fished and would often take me with them. They would carry me in and out of the boat, leaving my wheelchair on the shore. I loved watching my wheelchair get smaller and smaller the further we went out into the lake. We once watched as my chair slipped from a steep embankment into a river. We did not know whether to laugh or cry as Ernie jumped into the water in a successful attempt to retrieve it. I vividly recall how scared my niece, Tanya, was at the idea of losing my wheelchair, and how I did not care nearly as much as she did that I get it back. We all laugh about it at family functions now.

Furthermore, both Jim and my dad were national team athletes (my brother-in-law, Errol, was also an active competitor) in the sport of target shooting and I would often accompany them on trips to competitions; but, just like all my other physical activity and education experiences, I was left to watch from the sidelines. Coincidentally, around this same time, my dad met Richard, a small-motor mechanic who was a paraplegic. Knowing my dad's athletic history, he asked for some help in learning how to shoot. My dad provided him with equipment and some coaching. Once this fellow paraplegic started competing, Dad asked him if he knew of any young girls in wheelchairs who were involved in the sport. The answer was that there were not many, especially in Canada, but, nevertheless, this inspired Dad to encourage me to try. As it turned out, I had plenty of skill that surprised everyone, especially me. I loved shooting and it was a boost to my confidence that I was good at a sport. I was sixteen years old, it was 1986 and I attended several matches that year in competition against my non-disabled peers. While at Nationals that year I was approached and encouraged by Olympic gold medalist, Linda Thom, to try wheelchair sports. "You could be a Paralymic gold medalist," she told me. I retorted, "I plan to be an Olympic gold medalist, actually."

Despite my cheeky response, Linda's views strongly influenced my dad, who, while he acted as my coach and worked with me daily, continued to entice me with ideas about coaching and travel. Since target shooting is considered an inclusive sport in Canada, Dad took me to Calgary in the summer of 1987 to compete at the Nationals, where wheelchair shooting was included in the schedule of events. I was seventeen. This was my first ever exposure to other wheelchair shooters and to other people in wheelchairs in general. To persuade me to attend, my dad had bribed me with promises of shopping and allowing me to drive around a big city. I was just terribly reluctant to involve myself with other people in wheelchairs. As disability scholar Rosemarie Garland-Thomson posits, this reluctance I felt makes sense: "Our culture offers profound disincentives and few rewards to identifying as disabled."[10] I wrote this in my journal after my first event was over.

> These guys see me as just a girl. Before the match began, I even overheard one of them making the others laugh by asking them, "Can you shoot like a girl?" Well, I showed them how girls can shoot! I had a hard time getting into the range by myself and while bringing my equipment in I got stuck in the rain and was totally soaked before my first match. I was placed on the line right beside the current national champion, who looks like he has been shooting forever. He even had a beard for God's sake. I bet he was thinking, "Who the hell is she?" as I unpacked my gear and my lucky teddy bear. The rain had pooled in my chair and left a puddle underneath me. How embarrassing, but it also showed how tough I am. And I beat him. Not by much, but enough.

I earned membership on the national wheelchair team from that day of shooting, soaking wet, on the line. A few months later I was invited to attend the 1987 World Championships in Los Angeles, California.

Despite the promise of travelling to sunny and glamourous California, I was still extremely reluctant to associate myself with other wheelchair users. As disability theorist Carol Gill contends in her theory of disability identity development, many people who have disabilities have internalized the societal fear and devaluation of disability and have been socialized to reject people with disabilities as having something in common with them.[11] Gill argues that children with disabilities often communicate their wishes to feel like they belong by attending the same neighbourhood schools that "everyone else" does. She also states that some people with disabilities will "vigorously avoid"[12] contact with other people who have disabilities, especially activities that are primarily or exclusively for "the disabled" since they have internalized the stigma and public fear of disability. Before I met the team I would be working with, I was no exception to this. I vividly recall how nervous I was the day we first came together as a team at the Calgary International Airport as we were on our way to the World Championships in California, which was our first competition as a team. I had never been away from home on my own before. I had packed as much as possible into a carry-on duffle bag that I was hanging on to for dear life. I had not navigated an airport on my own before and I must have looked terrified. When we all came together in our pre-arranged meeting spot, the first thing I noticed was that aside from me, my team was made up entirely of men who were all older than me (I was seventeen) and that many of them were the men who had laughed at me a few months earlier in Calgary. It was the first time I had met our national coach, Finn Petersen. When I think about it now, being the only girl on an all-male team both helped and hindered my sexual identity development. It was strange for me, because for the first time my disability was not my primary identification with my teammates, as it had always been with everybody else. In the beginning of my shooting career my teammates did see me as female, but in a way that was a disadvantage. Because of my gender, I was an "added on" and reluctantly accepted part of the shooting team at first, not an immediately welcomed and included member of that team. They seemed suspicious of my skills, and I was so busy being nervous, that I am sure I did not seem warm and friendly. Their reluctance was less about what they did, after all, I was never left out of meetings or social gatherings or even sitting together during meals. In fact, we did everything together, a tactic that I credit Finn, our coach, with. He worked at creating a strong and cohesive team while treating each of us individually. I simply had the strong sense from my teammates that I needed to prove my abilities to them, to make them see that I was worth taking along. I remember once while at a combined training camp and competition at the Colorado Springs Olympic Training Center, the competitions were over and we had gathered in one of our rooms to play cards and cribbage. I curled up on a bunk and was almost asleep when I heard my teammates talking about me. I perked up my ears but did not open my eyes. When Finn steered the conversation to be not only respectful of my shooting skills but positive about my contribution to the team, my teammates followed suit. I was secretly pleased and felt like I had "arrived."

Similarly, when I had just turned nineteen and won two silver medals at the Paralympics in Seoul, Korea, in 1988, I felt that my status shifted in the eyes of my teammates from the derogatory "girl" to the inclusive "one of the boys." My teammates felt, I am sure, that there was no higher praise than to be labelled an honourary male. Because I had not felt like I had belonged anywhere before, being part of the team and described as "one of the boys" was an identification I accepted with open arms. I was used to not being seen as a girl and I was comfortable with that. Additionally, the sense of community I received from being part of a team was invaluable. We all had different personalities, yet we shared a love of laughing, pranks and telling jokes. We all adored Finn. We also shared similar body problems and needed similar accessibility because of our wheelchairs, and it was a combination of these things and much more that created an environment where I felt safe and, as Carol Gill would label, "at home."[13]

The fact that my team was made up of other wheelchair users like myself strongly shaped how I perceived having a disability and the meanings I gave it. Phenomenologist Maurice Merleau-Ponty argues that this group involvement is a revolutionary act of combating the oppressive structures.[14] Because of my involvement with these other people who had disabilities similar to my own, I created what Merleau-Ponty posits was a new way of identifying myself through my lived-body and by sharing that activity through the interaction of other individuals who were undergoing a similar transformative experience. With this drastic change in the way I felt about myself and the sense of community I was involved with, I made international competition a priority in my life. I enrolled in university part-time, but my priority was training and competing. Although my team lived in various parts of the country, we would attend training camps together, and travelling to different parts of the world for competitions was the norm. I trained every day and cross-trained with weights and various cardiovascular methods several times a week. During this time I did different sports as part of the cross-training, such as cross-country skiing and swimming. I kept in touch with Finn over the phone, but I still relied on my dad for regular coaching. I went on to win a bronze medal at the 1992 Paralympics in Barcelona, Spain.

I also won a drastic shift in identity. For one thing, the experience of high performance sport led me to see my body as having physical competence. Although Merleau-Ponty excludes the effect of differences like gender and disability from his analyses of embodiment, his description of motility nonetheless fits well here.[15] For him, motility is a belief that human subjectivity, or the ability to be insightful, perceptive and discerning, is a process not located in the mind, but rather in the body, and the ways in which your body moves in space is by consequence a new embodied experience. Since I was skilled at target shooting and was seen by my family members and coach as a strong and competitive athlete, I began to see my body in new, positive, competent and empowered ways. Finn also had a powerful influence on both my emotional and physical confidence. I stopped saying I was "in a wheelchair" and started calling myself a "wheelchair user," a label that gave me more power and control over my identity. I also began to see my wheelchair as a symbol of my strength and independence, rather than something that held me back. After all, I would say, "I do not get far without it." The perspectives on my sexual identity, and the expectations that surround those perspectives, however, did not really change. Through sport I began to see myself as strong and my body as skilled and physically competent, but there were still barriers to seeing myself as female.

I also won a community. Through my connection to my coach and teammates, as well as meeting many other people who used wheelchairs and had disabilities similar to mine, I became keenly interested in disability as a social construct. With my time in sport intersecting with my university studies, my scholarly pursuits became more and more disability-focused. I sought out any books or articles I could find on disabilities, I researched what accessibility efforts were going on at other universities, and I was always on the lookout for images of disability in the media and popular culture.

Girl Meets Boy

> *At last*
> *My love has come along*
> *My lonely days are over*
> *and life is like a song*
> *(Etta James, "At Last")*

It was during this time that I also met, and eventually married, my husband, Darrell. We met in high school because we had the same homeroom, were in many of the same classes and shared some of the same friends. Upon reflection, it was not easy for Darrell to get close to me. I had bought into the idea that I was not feminine or certainly not feminine or pretty enough to be date-worthy. He spent a lot of time convincing me otherwise and took great pains to take me places that had been previously off limits (in those days, he carried me up a lot of stairs to parties, and in and out of his parents' house). One event that particularly sticks out in my mind was when our high school's football team went to provincial championships in Regina. I wanted to attend the game but believed I would need my parents to drive me there since I could not get on the chartered school bus that everyone else would be travelling on. Darrell insisted on the two of us getting on that bus (he carried me on and off and made a place for my wheelchair to be stored) and travelling the four-hour ride with everyone else. I was self-conscious and I worried about what people were thinking and saying, and yet, I was proud to sit there with him. Despite how strong I knew he was (he also had a part-time job delivering furniture), I remember feeling uneasy about him carrying me around. The first time I told him I was nervous that I was too heavy for him, he replied, "Don't worry, you're lighter than a refrigerator." I pretended to be offended; he just laughed.

Darrell was always confident about his choice to be with me. He would tell me that the wheelchair was secondary to our relationship, and yet, it was such an important part of who I was that he had trouble seeing me without it. And right from the beginning, he admitted to imagining a long future ahead of us, and so, I began to imagine it too.

This is important to note, because until Darrell and I started dating, I did not have much of an imagination for my adult life. I thought I would be a writer, but I did not envision someone hiring me to do anything, or getting married, or having kids. Although I was not expected to attend my junior high or high school dances, I went anyway, and the reason was simple. I loved music and could not help myself from moving to it. Although I had friends, and a few friends who were boys (very few) who would dance with me, I was quite self-conscious about attending school dances. I wondered if people thought I did not deserve to be there. Even before we started dating, Darrell was one of those boys who would dance with me. During one particular high school dance, we attempted a slow dance together, which takes imagination when a wheelchair is between two people. He ended up half-sitting on my lap, and when we kissed on the dance floor, the people who were dancing around us stopped and stared. Although I was focused on the moment, I was also worried about how Darrell might be embarrassed, how he might reject me, and instead, he just seemed to block everyone else out. It was not long after that when he began hinting that we were made for each other.

I am embarrassed to admit it now, but I needed a lot of reassurance. For a long time during our courtship I was suspicious about what he found attractive about me. He had astonishingly blue eyes and a smile that was anchored by the deepest dimples I had ever seen. He had all the qualities of a great boyfriend: he was attractive, smart, funny, kind and friendly. He was the kind of boy who could be with anyone he wanted. Therefore, I wondered why he wanted to be with me. I would try to "catch" him having negative attitudes about my paralysis and my wheelchair. When I once asked Darrell what the first thing he ever noticed about me was (expecting he would say my wheelchair and thus make me correct in my assumptions that my disability was "in the way" of our relationship) and he replied without hesitation, "I noticed your sunburn," I finally allowed myself to fall head over heels. When I look back on that time, I marvel over how he defied social expectations and how much of a social risk he took by dating me. The reason I am convinced of his bravery is simple: although in our graduating class of nearly 300 people I had a lot of friends who were boys who would have lunch with me, hang out with me during our "spares" and party with me on the weekends, most of those same boys were reluctant to dance with me at a school dance and none of them, at least to my knowledge, would consider dating me.

Not the Girl Next Door

My disability often rendered me sexless and genderless in the eyes of others. I had girlfriends, but I was constantly aware of my "supportive" role within many of those friendships. When we were sixteen, my one friend declared she had a terrible crush on the same boy that I secretly liked. Once I learned this, I made the decision to not make my crush known to her. Because I was not a perceived "threat" to stealing boys away from my peers, I think I had the advantage of making more friends without the nastiness and jealousies that sometimes occurs with groups of girls. Garland-Thomson clearly states that "banishment from femininity can be both a liability and a benefit,"[16] and this was certainly my experience in high school. While it is true that my genderless identity did make me un-dateable in the eyes of many boys, at the same time, my non-threatening and almost chameleon-like identity allowed me to make connections with many of the strongly formed "cliques" in our school. I was friendly with leaders, geeks, jocks, druggies and loners. The advantage of having so many friends allowed for enough votes to win me the class president election — a shared role between a girl and a boy named "Senior Pin" and "Senior Ring." I ran in the election because I was convinced that if I worked hard enough and involved myself in school activities (which might be seen as "overachieving" to some), I could maybe be seen as on an equal playing field with my peers. My motives were never to overachieve; my motives were to be like everyone else.

Despite my role as co-president and my unconventional popularity (the traditionally popular people were good-looking and fit, as I suspect they are in most high schools even now), I was not considered a social commodity. Yes, I was welcome at the parties but I was not expected to get together with a boy or meet a boy at one of those parties. There was an unspoken assumption that I would not be getting involved in the social/dating/romantic scene that my peers were. So imagine the social code that was broken when Darrell was seen dating me, kissing me in the hallway and holding my hand during library time. One friend confided in me that "everyone" was talking about how incredible it was that Darrell and I were "going out" and the gossip and speculation that our relationship would not last. I also heard from another friend that she had it on good authority that even the teachers were talking about it. I do not know if that is true or not, but I do know that we were a surprise couple to many. When I recently asked Darrell about it to help me piece this part of the story together, he simply brushed it off, saying it was "no big thing." Whether it was or it was not a big thing is maybe not the point. All I knew is that I had never felt so understood, or so meaningfully connected to anyone before. I also remain convinced of how both his bravery and strong sense of self enabled us to come together. He was happy with me, he was not bothered by the reactions of others and, consequently, we were busy having too much fun to be overly introspective. The act Darrell took in dating me was one of stepping outside firmly established social norms.

We were married two years after high school, in 1989. I was told by some of our high school friends who attended that some people showed up at the church uninvited just to see if "Darrell went through with it." For our wedding, my mom (with help from my grandma) made me a spectacular ivory chiffon dress with a skirt so full it covered up half my wheelchair. My mom even covered the black upholstery of my wheelchair with the same material as my wedding dress. During our first dance, Darrell surprised me (and most everyone in attendance) by taking off his tuxedo jacket, lifting me out of my chair and carrying me around the dance floor while the whoops and hollers of our friends and family nearly drowned out the music of our song: "Why Worry" by Dire Straits. This time we got the slow dance right. While it is not a typical love song, what we chose to dance to fit with our non-typical relationship. The melody was graceful and soothing and the words are meaningful and comforting, even now, almost twenty years later:

> Why worry, there should be laughter after pain
> There should be sunshine after rain
> (Dire Straits, "Why Worry")

I am flabbergasted at how unprepared we were for married life. There were so many strikes against us: we were high school sweethearts; although Darrell was working, I did not have a job and was taking a few university courses and attempting to make money by freelance writing. I was training and competing, which was also a drain on our finances; we had a small apartment furnished by cast-offs and hand-me-downs. We had no plans for our future and we had no savings. Yet, we were happy. Our marriage never should have worked for all these reasons and more. However, we just focused on being together and stayed committed to growing and changing together.

It was only after about a year that we both started attending university with more seriousness. I was still competing and Darrell was still working while we studied. Eventually we moved to Saskatoon to become full-time students. I can still see my parents waving to us from their farmhouse doorstep as we said goodbye. Although I had not lived in their house for a few years, it was still painful to leave and to let go. Moving away to another city somehow felt like a significant marking of my adult life, even more than getting married. As we drove away, I remember crying and holding Darrell's hand, feeling scared but excited about the possibilities ahead. It is fair to say that our university experience transformed us as individuals and as a couple. Our world views broadened and our love for learning blossomed.

'Cause we've got stayin' power
You and I
Stayin' power through thick and thin
(Neil Young, "Stayin' Power")

Finding My Inner Girl

At the time that I write this, Darrell and I have been married twenty years. I recently delivered a guest lecture on my perspectives on mothering with a disability and I was asked by one of the students how my relationship with my husband influenced my sexual identity. This student explained that she assumed that simply once I had a sexual relationship, surely I then saw myself as sexual. My response was, yes, that was true. My connection with Darrell was an intensely important part of my development and sexual identity, and yet, at the same time, I still did not feel innately sexual. My romantic and loving relationship with my husband definitely helped me with my views on how I defined myself as female, but his validation of my worth as a sexual person was still external to my inner core and my intrinsic feelings of femininity. Simply put, his love of me and my body were not enough. I needed to experience an embodied change as dramatic and altering as pregnancy and childbirth in order to finally see that I am a woman. One of the questions that non-disabled people admit to is wondering secretly about whether or not people with disabilities have sex. Darrell could kiss or hug me in public, which may have provided part of the answer to this curiosity, but when I was obviously pregnant, those curiousities were answered: yes, I can, and do, have sex. And that mattered to me, probably more than it should. But I admit that it did.

These feelings make sense when I consider the literature on how becoming pregnant can prompt a shift in the ways women identify themselves. Becoming a mother often means a re-evaluation of one's body.[17] Because bodies with disabilities are often seen for what they cannot do, taking on the role of mother can give the body a different value, status and worth.[18] Grue and Laerum also found that for women who were injured in childhood, or who have lived with their disabilities all their lives, becoming a mother often gave women an opportunity to reclaim their lost or absent sexual identities. As I reflect on my relationship with Darrell, I suspect that the privacy of our sexual relationship did not adequately allow me to believe in and trust my sexuality. When he was open with affection for me in public, I was certainly validated as a sexual and even pretty woman. On the other hand, when I was obviously pregnant, my body was open for public presentation, and therefore no one could deny my sexuality and femininity, not even me.

August 17, 1996

> Mother. Pregnancy. Parent. I never expected these roles for myself. These roles were never expected for me. How am I going to do this right when it was never in the imagination for what is possible?

These days, when I read the above passage, I am not sure what I meant by "right." While I do not believe that there is a right way to be pregnant, give birth and be a mother, there nevertheless exists a societal expectation that, once pregnant, women's bodies are open for public scrutiny more than they ever were prior to being pregnant. In particular, it is such an ingrained societal expectation that pregnant women are doing everything in their power to have a "healthy" pregnancy that there is no alternative perception available on this issue. New Zealand researcher and writer Robyn Longhurst suggests that this is part of an array of "normative expectations" that prescribe how women will do pregnancy the "right" way.[19] Sociologist Alexandra Howson agrees and also argues that these surveillance practices, like pre-natal care, are so much a part of our social consciousness that we completely take them for granted.[20] Other feminist writers, such as Rosalyn Diprose, have addressed how bodies (especially female bodies) are open for public scrutiny and how the pregnant body is constantly under surveillance.[21] Sociologist Carol Thomas argues that women with disabilities are particularly vulnerable to this scrutiny.[22]

The public scrutiny that Thomas writes about makes me think about a particular memory of mine when I became pregnant with Patrick. I was twenty-seven years old and working full-time as the manager of Disability Services for Students at the University of Saskatchewan. Because Finn had retired from coaching, I took an extended break from shooting to finish my degree and start working. Despite the fact that I had read anything I could get my hands on about disabilities, both for the purposes of work as well as my burgeoning personal interest, I still spent weeks and weeks in disbelief that my disabled body was actually growing a baby and I was overwhelmed daily with fears of how I would be scrutinized by others. I spoke to one of my doctors about how frightened I was, how I lacked confidence and how difficult it was to accept that something was happening to me that I never imagined would. While what I actually needed was an encouraging word and help making connections with other paraplegic mothers, my doctor instead mistook my symptoms to be depression and gently suggested that I should have a "therapeutic" abortion. As I learned later on, women with disabilities frequently miss out on supportive health care during their pregnancies and therefore some of them even receive strong suggestions to abort their fetuses.[23]

The public scrutiny and the unhelpful advice from health-care professionals should not have come as a surprise to me. There are few examples of women with disabilities in stereotypical situations. However, when we were first married, Darrell bought me a real Barbie doll named Becky who used a red wheelchair. He gave me this doll when I was as a university student and women's and gender studies classes were widening my thoughts and reflections on my sexuality and my femininity. I immediately loved that doll and I still treasure her today, as do both my children who still play with her. When Darrell handed me the trademark bright pink box, I remember saying out loud how differently my life might have been if such a toy had existed when I was a young girl. I might have been able to see myself reflected in society, in my community, my school and in my peer group. After all, my environment was devoid of other people with disabilities. Furthermore, I now see that my situation was more complex than that. While it is true that my community lacked other children or grown-ups who used wheelchairs, what is also true is that the overriding culture is an invisible and pervasively able-bodied one.[24] It is only very recently that I see that these two things are not one and the same.

Of particular interest to me is the idea of the able-bodied environment, the pervasive able-bodied ideology and ubiquitous pro-ability culture that hates everything disabled.[25] Garland-Thomson draws comparisons between disability and race, using Pulitzer-prize winning author Toni Morrison's 1970 novel *The Bluest Eye* as an example. *The Bluest Eye* heightened my interest in the race-disability comparison. *The Bluest Eye* is a story about a little black girl named Pecola who loves blue eyes; white images are everywhere, from the films shown in the local movie theatres, to the nicknames "Ginger Rogers" and "Greta Garbo" that the adult men give to the little girls, to the white blue-eyed dolls those black girls receive as gifts. So strong is the white ideology, Pecola prays for her own eyes to change from brown to blue, believing that, if they did, all her problems would vanish and she would be left with a wonderful life. In the story there are no white people telling Percola that she is ugly and that she needs to be blond-haired and blue-eyed in order to be acceptable and loveable; rather, Morrison reaches beyond this work of literature to speak to how a racist social system is so all-encompassing that dominant images of whiteness show young black children that to be white means to be successful and happy. When those same black children then look around at their own lives of poverty and oppression, they learn to hate their black heritage for keeping them from the Shirley Temple world.

I include this brief analysis of the novel because I believe that Pecola's beliefs and desires to look white, blond and blue-eyed are similar to my own feelings of wanting to be able to look and feel more like my non-disabled peers when I was a little girl. I think that although no one was telling me that being paralyzed made me unlovable and unacceptable, the ideas of disability as a pervasive social ideology strongly informed my ideas of who I was.[26]

For me, receiving a doll that had a wheelchair would have meant that someone (particularly "someone" as large as the Mattel Corporation) had seen disability as acceptable and worthy of inclusion. Sometimes, something as simple as a doll really can make a difference in how a child sees herself mirrored in the world. Similarly, I think I would have experienced my future maternal roles more confidently if I had been able to read another disabled woman's story about her pregnancy and childbirth. I had listened to my sister, my friends and my cousins talk about what childbirth was like, but I did not think their experiences would apply to me because their bodies were not like mine. I think my mom wanted to believe that I could have a baby but was afraid to admit it out loud. In fact, when I told her the news, she said she had suspected but was scared that if she asked, only to hear that I was not pregnant, she would have disappointed and hurt me. None of us had heard about anyone with a spinal cord injury who had a baby, plain and simple. I think both myself and the medical professionals who worked with me would have been better prepared if we had all had access to more information, research and testimony about how disability, pregnancy and childbirth can intersect. Just as I do not look like Becky (the wheelchair and the red sneakers she wears are our only real commonalities — who really looks like Barbie, after all?), I do not expect that my story will ever be a direct comparison to someone else's. However, I still believe that sharing my story can make a difference for women with disabilities who want to have children, for the parents and partners of those women and for anyone who has ever lived with a complicated body or a complicated life and who needs to know that possibilities exist. Amy Mullin argues that the study of both non-disabled and disabled women's experiences with pregnancy is both rare and new and not enough is known about how it affects a woman's sense of herself as a female.[27] Mullin also argues that because pregnancy is such a meaningful embodied experience, it is important to look at all kinds of contexts (e.g., social, cultural) because there will not be "such a thing as a typical experience of pregnancy."[28] I know that when I was pregnant I would have liked to know I was not alone.

Big Girls Don't Cry

This book actually began as the thesis I wrote using the method of "autoethnography" as part of the necessary requirements for a master's of science degree in kinesiology. Because an autoethnography is a personal story interweaved with theory and broader social issues, I think the method allowed me to develop deeper understandings of disability, pregnancy and childbirth. It is my wish that my writing also enables readers — with or without disabilities — to see themselves reflected in my story.

When it came to writing this book, I had to make many decisions about what is private and what is public. For example, I could have chosen to just protect the stories from public eye forever, leaving my journals for my children to find and read someday. For another, I had to decide what stories are written down, which stories stay and which ones leave. While technological advances such as blogging and social media networking encourage a great deal more self disclosure than our society has probably ever previously witnessed, I think privacy still matters in this world. Darrell helped me decide where our boundaries should be, but for the most part the choices were mine alone. And yet, at the same time, it is almost as though some of the stories have lives of their own. They want out. They insist. Writing them down can be a mechanical process at times, but most other times it is a painful embodied process containing an aching chest, a nauseous stomach and eruptive tears. It is difficult during emotional moments like these to even think straight, and yet, miraculously, my fingers nevertheless just keep putting down the words. During these times they insist on breaking the silence by typing despite my emotional response. So despite all my consciously made choices, I also recognize that there is a story, or a collection of many stories, here that have been unheard for too long and that, in the telling, have the ability to bring about change. They can change attitudes about what it means to have a disability. They can educate medical professionals. But what I hope for most is that these stories can give strength and hope to other people with disabilities who want to experience all the depth, richness, complexity and reward that can only come from the experience of loving a child.

2

Thinking and Writing about Myself

When my whole life is on the tip of my tongue ...
You hear me say, each life has its place
(Indigo Girls, "Virginia Woolf")

During the time that I wrote my thesis that is now this book, I participated in a Life and Health Sciences Research Day held for graduate students at the University of Saskatchewan. Each participant displayed his or her research in poster form and had the opportunity to give a five-minute speech to a team of judges. All posters and presentations were evaluated and prizes were awarded at the end of the day.

I had not anticipated how few numbers of qualitative research projects were present at the event, but nevertheless when it was my turn to speak about my own project, I believe I did so with confidence and enthusiasm. At the end of the day when I was awarded second place in my category, I suspected that the award was a reflection of my public speaking skills and less about the perceived quality of my research. After all, my judges were honest — although they were genuinely intrigued by my story, they could not see the scientific significance. One judge asked me, "Why didn't you choose to write an autobiography or a memoir and skip the academic exercise altogether?" Thinking about how emotional the writing, remembering and reflecting process had been, I laughed and answered honestly, "I have asked myself that question many times." What graduate student, after all, at some point does not question his or her decision to continue on the path of graduate studies, which can be frustrating, difficult, lonely and financially challenging? The judge then further pressed, "What is the point of doing this academic exercise if the work does not generalize and therefore does not apply to anyone else but you?"

Good questions. To answer his first query, I choose to persevere through the academic exercise because of my desire to create social change about how disabilities are perceived and how women with disabilities can be seen as competent nurturers. My perseverance was grounded in the realization that while there is no shortage of literature that examines female bodies, whether the writing is popular or academic, much of the literature that examines the female bodily experience excludes the stories and experiences of women with disabilities.[1] Undoubtedly, discursive analyses of women's embodied experiences and pregnancy have been embraced by feminist scholars.[2] Still, feminist research has also neglected the embodiment issues, including pregnancy, of women with disabilities.[3] Disability theorist, Tonya Titchkosky, says "Disability has typically been left out of the politics and theorizing of gender."[4] Disability scholar Susan Wendell, whose writings have been enormously influential on my own work, argues that because feminist movements have focused attention on women's strength and celebrated the experiences of women's bodies that give pleasure, they have also overlooked embodiment differences, particularly disabilities.[5] Some disability activists, like Carol Gill, believe that the feminist movement has made efforts to include many other "differences" into their activism, but continually neglects women with disabilities, choosing rather to see this group of women as having diminished societal value.[6] Feminist research has also focused on the objectification of women's bodies as sources of exploitation, but has undervalued and repeatedly excluded the female body with disabilities, and bodies that are not traditionally considered sexual, competent or physically strong. Susan Wendell says it so well: "Until feminists criticize our own body ideals and confront the weak, suffering, and uncontrollable body in our theorizing and practice, women with disabilities and illnesses are likely to feel that we are embarrassments to feminism."[7]

As a graduate student beginning her studies, I had read about qualitative inquiry to give myself a solid grounding in methodologies and I began to have a desire to influence higher learning. I also came to recognize that it is important that people with disabilities are active in research processes, since research in the area of disability has often been done by "outsiders" — those who do not share the disability experience.[8] I realized that I had a desire to reach and inform doctors, nurses and students of the health sciences with my story so that they could re-think the way they practise medicine. As my thesis progressed, I remained committed to the writing through a desire to contribute to the larger conceptual and theoretical understandings of disability in our society. I was extremely grateful for the literature on disability that I found. I learned through my work with Disability Services that while sometimes accessibility in terms of renovations or adaptive technology costs money, other times lives could be changed by small acts — acts of compassion and understanding. Similarly, my research led me to see the power of the singular voice. Large and powerful theories were not the only things that changed the way I saw disability. Often, all I needed was one story. For example, my life, the way I saw my life, was transformed when I read the essay "On Being a Cripple" by disability feminist writer, Nancy Mairs, who has multiple sclerosis. I was forever changed after reading *The Breast Cancer Journals* by Audre Lorde. Lorde overtly challenged me to live a considered life, but through her words she also compelled me to write my life. And so it was on the difficult days of writing this book that I remained grounded through my faith that telling my own personal story can also make bigger points about our social condition, and I tried to make those points by contrasting my stories against a social environment that tends to be ableist.

While I wrote, I kept the hope that by telling this story of disability I was putting a face on disability issues, illuminating the social oppression that exists for people with disabilities, offering solutions to those problems and presenting another way of thinking and acting. In some ways, it is one thing for a woman to live a considered life by reflecting on her own life and making it better. For me, the moments of tremendous personal growth and change happened when other women put forward their considered lives and, by doing that, helped me to grow, change and become an activist. Simply, I came to believe that if I was not willing to be part of the narrative, I was part of the problem. Today, I am driven to be part of a change for people with disabilities, for improved accessibility and to change negative and misinformed perceptions and attitudes.

To answer my judge's second question, I believe that my story is not just about me. First of all, disability is a pervasive ideology that informs many of our cultural ideas of self and other, as well as what constitutes acceptable and celebratory bodies, political stances, public policy and language.[9] Autoethnography allowed me, as qualitative researcher Deborah Reed-Danahay explains, to write a self-narrative that placed those stories within a social context.[10] And although my story will not be exactly the same as another non-disabled woman's or even another female paraplegic's story, by intertwining my story with larger theories and understandings of disability it can inform others about the ways in which disability is seen, heard, felt and experienced.

I also think that my writing could reach further than the circle of women with disabilities and help to inform anyone about what it is like to live with vulnerabilities, injuries, weakness, pain, interruption and compromise. Becoming sick, injured or in need of medical intervention and even possibly hospitalization is a situation experienced by almost everyone. Despite our efforts for optimum health, strength and fitness, all bodies experience vulnerability and even disability at some point in their lives. Disability, in all its varying forms and degrees, is a human experience that can affect anyone. As disability theorist Susan Wendell asserts, the experience of disability, while often considered atypical, by necessity extends the range of possible human physical experiences in ways not available to the able-bodied human population.[11] A more complete understanding of embodiment requires a thorough understanding of the bodily experience of disability. Susan Wendell further argues that in order to grasp the relationship of consciousness to the body, it is essential to understand the embodied experiences of women with physical disabilities.[12] Other disability academics agree. For example, Michael Berube argues that the subject of disability "will be central to human existence for as long as humans have bodies — and embodied minds to theorize them with."[13] Tonya Titchkosky writes, "I hold that the problematic of 'embodiment,' of fleshy life, of our being embodied beings, can be grasped through an analysis of how we give meaning to disability within everyday life."[14] Moreover, as Rosemarie Garland-Thomson states, "disability is the most human of experiences, touching every family, and — if we live long enough — touching us all."[15] Perhaps, then, my research is not as unique as it seems.

More than Just a Story

> *A story about a girl*
> *A story about the world*
> *(Our Lady Peace, "A Story about a Girl")*

An important part of understanding disabilities must come from an individual experience and the stories we tell. Stories are an important way of bringing understanding to the lives of those from whom we otherwise do not hear. Qualitative researcher Tami Muncey writes that there are "lots more stories waiting to be told, stories that are sometimes difficult to tell, that need support and understanding in the telling."[16] However, I wanted to do more than just tell a story. My goal was to connect the personal story to the cultural, situating the self within, and yet apart from, a social context — therefore flowing from a personal perspective to a cultural or societal one and back again.

Bodies

> *At times I just don't know*
> *how you could be anything but beautiful*
> *(Gordon Lightfoot, "Beautiful")*

The body is a beautiful source of knowledge and all our bodies have stories to tell. Pathologized bodies and bodies that have experienced disability and illness have stories that rarely get told. The experience of pregnancy and childbirth was particularly life-changing for me, and because I have always felt compelled to write down the stories of my life, I documented these experiences with my two children throughout several handwritten journals. I feel that these stories, my lived experiences as a woman with a disability experiencing pregnancy, offer insights and understanding into what is already known about women's bodies.

It is important that experiences from those who live in "different" bodies and are living "different" experiences are uncovered. Hearing the disability experience has the potential to empower people with disabilities but it also helps us understand what it means to live embodied in the world. As Susan Wendell asserts, the experience of disability expands the variety of possible human physical experiences that the able-bodied human population may never experience.[17] A more complete understanding of embodiment therefore then requires a comprehensive understanding of the embodied experience of disability.

Looking Inward/Looking Outward

I know there is strength in the differences between us
And I know there is comfort where we overlap
(ani difranco, "Overlap")

This book is not just an autobiography in that it "connect(s) the autobiographical and personal to the cultural and social."[18] This kind of writing and thinking can encourage empathy and connection beyond the self and contribute to meaningful sociological understandings.[19]

A good way to understand this way of looking inward and gazing outward is to look at an example. In his work "The Fatal Flaw: A Narrative of the Fragile Body-Self," Andrew Sparkes describes what it was like to define himself as an elite athlete and have both his athleticism and regular life activities interrupted when inflammatory back disease became a part of his daily life.[20] He writes: "I… attempt to take you as the reader into the intimacies of my world. I hope to do this in such a way that you are stimulated to reflect upon your own life in relation to mine."[21] Andrew Sparkes' reflections on athleticism resonated with me. Having several years of experience in high performance target shooting, I like to think of the personal and cultural components of autoethnography in comparison to shooting an air pistol. When a shooter peers through the sights of an air pistol he or she can clearly see either the front sight, which is directly in front of him or her (the personal), or the target, which is down range ten meters away (the cultural). A skilled shooter creates a picture of both of these and, depending on where he or she is at in the process of releasing the shot, either the sights or the target will be emphasized and sharply seen, but both must and will be part of the image. "Autoethnography is setting a scene, telling a story, weaving intricate connections among life and art, experience and theory, evocation and explanation… and then letting go, hoping for readers who will bring the same careful attention to your words in the context of their own lives."[22]

Keeping Track of My Life: Journals

They published your diary
and that's how I got to know you
(Indigo Girls, "Virginia Woolf")

The process of writing my life is not new to me, as I have been writing for over twenty-five years. As a child, writing was a way to keep myself "company" on those lonely days in the hospital. When I was a young girl, I called these books my diaries. As a teenager I started to call them journals, which felt like a more sophisticated and mature label. For me now, the difference between a diary and a journal is one of focused content. A journal is a place where I can explore my thoughts, my feelings and my questions about life. A diary, at least for me, is a place where events are recorded in a specific place and time. My journal holds some day-to-day events, such as documenting my children's birthdays or the anniversary of my car accident. However, my journal also contains lists of things I want to do while I am still lucky enough to be alive, the songs that I consider to be the soundtrack of my life, and my anticipations and fears about growing old. My journal writing these days contains fewer day-to-day accounts and, instead, more about the nuggets of meaningful interactions or thoughts I had during a day. As a writer of personalized essays, Joan Didion has much to say about the purpose of keeping a "notebook" or journal. She agrees with my lack of interest in keeping a log of the day's events, saying, "Who cares?" She, like me, would much rather dissect the day's moments, writing down what influences and inspires instead.

Whatever the label — diary, notebook or journal — writing in small, blank books when I was a little girl was a way to tell my secrets, since many of my childhood experiences, particularly those times spent in the hospital, were not always positive and happy. My journals were my friends because I trusted them with my secretive stories and they therefore became one of my main means of coping. As a teenager and in my early adult years, the writing process gradually evolved to became one of self-reflection, even therapy. Phenomenologist Max van Manen captures my reason for journaling: "Intensive journal writing is used for the purpose of 'self-discovery' or for coming to terms with personal problems or issues in one's private life."[23]

Writing became a compulsion. Keeping a journal helped to fill the sense that I was missing something. When I wrote, I think the stories that ended up on the pages provided me with a kind of proof that I have a life worth living. Later on, I started to look at my journals in another way. I wondered if they could contribute to our meanings of bodies, of what it means to be a woman, and of what it means to be a woman with a disability.

Collect what we say and what we save to discard
and discover a brand new way
(Tegan and Sara, "Hell")

The journal entries from which I drew the stories of pregnancy, childbirth and disability were the ones I started on the day I learned I was pregnant with each of my children and ended on the days I gave birth to them. Some other stories are included in this book, such as those from my childhood and my time with sports. Although I eventually had to limit how much I went back through the years of journal entries, I found that a few pivotal experiences from other times in my life besides the times I was pregnant, were key to putting this all together.

Other people have done similar kinds of writing. For example, Elizabeth Ettore wrote her story in diaries that she kept for two years while living with a chronic illness.[24] She also attached letters to her diary entries. Before writing, she thoroughly read her diaries several times. She then wrote down the key events in a chronological order. Ettore found that engaging in this process is painful and emotional, and yet she writes that it was in this painful introspection where she found healing and the chance to make sense of her illness experience. I used a similar process of reading and re-reading, writing down key events in a chronological order and determining the themes. The process of categorization and creating themes changed again once I started writing. What was surprising was how the best stories emerged in a much messier way than I could have ever anticipated. Themes and sub-themes were revealed to me at my desk, but also at unexpected times during the course of a day.

I used other journals in addition to those about my pregnancy and birthing. During the process of finding the themes and the most meaningful stories, especially when I wrote down a timeline of key events in my life, I remembered yet more stories. I re-read my pregnancy journal entries at least six, if not more, times. The process of transcribing involved another reading. Through the process of reading my journals and transcribing them, I experienced some of the introspective pain that Ettore describes. I considered quitting more than once. I had heard about other students who had attempted autoethnography but quit because the process of writing and remembering was too emotionally taxing. I could relate.

Interestingly, exploring my personal story against the landscape of disability theory and feminist theory connected it to the larger cultural and social context, which made the painful introspection easier to take. Perhaps this was because I felt my experiences were given validity and legitimacy and that writing them in this way had the potential to contribute to a "higher purpose."

Music Lyrics

Music is a world within itself
with a language we all understand
With an equal opportunity
for all to sing, dance, and clap their hands
(Stevie Wonder, "Sir Duke")

Like many people, I simply love music. Music nourishes me and gives me energy. This has been the case ever since I can remember, whether the music came from my mother's many songs that she would spontaneously break out in whenever she was inspired (which was often), the many songs my dad would whistle or the countless popular songs from the 1970s that my brother, Jim, would introduce me to on his 8-track stereo. It was not unusual to watch my mom dance a little jig in the kitchen while she worked or to secretly witness my parents dancing to a waltz in the living room after dark. These days, I am always on the search for new, often local, independent and "alternative" music to listen to. Patrick plays a few instruments; I also dabble in playing the guitar and the piano. I sing, well or otherwise, every day.

Music lyrics are forms of art that give me feelings of connection in the social world. I have collected music lyrics that "speak to me" for over twenty years and these lyrics help to tell my story. Some of the lyrics I used in this book are ones that I have captured in my journals, some are posted on the bulletin board in my office, and still others are kept on scrap pieces of paper in my wallet. During the writing of this book, I started keeping electronic files of music that was important to me. The collection is eclectic. Many of the lyrics that I collect are written by women singer/songwriters or are songs by both men and women about social justice and fairness. Some are by popular music artists, others are more obscure and lesser known. It felt both natural and critical that some of them are included in the telling of my personal story because they are a part of who I am and who I consider myself to be to others. I think they give my book beauty.

We all need beauty. We cannot thrive or survive without it, and this is one of the many things that the arts give to our lives, and this is what music gives to me. The music lyrics in this book, many of which are written (and performed) by women, added a piece to this puzzle of my experience with pregnancy, childbirth and disability. According to author Charlotte Greig, this makes sense. She writes that the presence of women songwriters who disclose their experiences with femininity, identity, childbearing and motherhood has an impact in how women listeners see themselves and their own experiences.[25] The connection I felt to music lyrics during my pregnancy and childbirth was significant to my experience. I needed to hear what other women thought about motherhood and reflect on whether their words described my own thoughts. I felt compelled to find music that made me feel connected to other women because, while pregnant, I was feeling like a woman for the first time in many ways. For these reasons and many others, music simply helped me make sense of my experience

I also included music, written by both men and women, that reflected themes of social fairness and that spoke out against social injustice. These themes resonated with me due to the difficulties I was experiencing with my doctor, the inaccessibility of the hospital, my own conflict about my identity and expectations and the negative attitudes others had of my pregnancies and childbirths. I was also often inspired by music lyrics during the writing of this book. Sometimes I sought out the lyrics, but most of the time they found me. Charlotte Greig echoes my feelings of connection when she writes that music can make a listener feel like she is part of a community of those who share dilemmas, problems and decisions.[26]

Adding music lyrics allowed me to reflect on how I make decisions, how songs resonate with me, and the process by which I make decisions about which parts of a song to use and which parts I leave behind. The whole practice of contemplation, decision-making and interpretation of music lyrics was one I found intriguing. Music theorist Anthony Pople (1994) asserts that there is no "real" meaning in theory and that we all use different ways to emphasize and combine meanings for our own purposes.[27] In this light, there is no "true" meaning in a song. For example, "Change Is Gonna Come," a famous song by Sam Cooke that was originally intended as a protest and commentary about racism in 1960s America, reverberates with meaning for me — a white Canadian woman with a disability. The meanings of the lyrics I chose are interpreted, constructed and even re-written through the lens of how I interpret, construct and re-write my own life, my own self.

> *Truth is fiction*
> *Truth is lies*
> *Strange things happen when worlds collide*
> *(Neil Young, "When Worlds Collide")*

Letters to Sharon

As a young girl, I was a letter writer and had several pen-pals, especially in Western Canada, due to my involvement as a creative writer for one of our agricultural newspapers. Years later, when physiotherapist-turned-trusted and dear friend, Sharon, embarked on a trip that physically separated us for several months, we started writing letters to each other. Later, when she re-located to another city, we continued writing and have never really stopped. Sharon kept all my letters (as I kept hers) and, knowing I would appreciate the gesture, she returned them to me when she was packing and moving to a new home.

> **From:** Heather Kuttai
>
> **Sent:** April 13, 2007 10:07 PM
>
> **To:** Donna Goodwin
>
> **Subject:** the lottery
>
> I feel like I just won it.
>
> I read another 2 new journal articles (one by Duncan, one by Ward) on autoethnography today. One of them just briefly mentioned other artifacts and named letters in the long list. A huge light bulb went off.
>
> My former physiotherapist and now very close friend, Sharon, and I exchanged letters for years. About 5 years ago she sent all of mine back to me with a note saying that she had the feeling I might need them someday. She was right. I wrote her at least once a month while I was pregnant with Patrick. The fact that she was my physio is relevant – we had a close relationship that centred around my body. Furthermore, she went through a life change by leaving her husband for another woman (with whom she has been in a long time relationship – over 10 years) and those themes are important because we were, in these letters, exploring our new identities as women together. These letters will definitely be part of my data.
>
> Don't you love it when the stars just line right up for you?
>
> Had to share. Talk to you soon.
>
> hk

As I said in my email to Donna, I knew the letters would contribute to my story and provide another dimension to how I was thinking and feeling during my pregnancies. Therefore, I transcribed eight letters I wrote to Sharon during my first pregnancy.

While my journal entries provided the main body of my data, the letters take on another angle of my story because of whom I wrote them to. Ever since I took English 270 as an undergraduate student, I have been interested in the concept of audience in forms of life writing. I read Anne Frank's famous diaries with the question of whom she was writing to — a friend, her version of God, herself? When words are put down on paper, I think the writer is aware that someone, someday, may read those words and, thus, an audience is present. My letters to Sharon speak to this idea. I disclosed experiences and feelings differently to her than I would in my "private" journal.

Building My Book Out of Glass

> *I build each one of my songs out of glass*
> *so you can see me inside them I suppose*
> *Or you could just leave the image of me*
> *and watch your own reflection*
> *(ani difranco, "Overlap")*

With reflective stories, journal entries and connections to social contexts, my intent was to "build this book out of glass." With an authentic and transparent voice, I want you to be able to clearly see me and my experiences with pregnancy, childbirth and disability. I also want you to be able to "leave the image of me in the background" so that you can see your own life in new and unexpected ways.

3

In the Family Way

October 7, 1996

…we were soon then ushered to our ultrasound. And I discovered the most amazing thing: there really is a baby in there, in here, in me. We saw it. Its head, body, arms, legs, heart. Its spine, hip bones, stomach. And it raised its hand to us, as though it was waving. The woman doing the ultrasound said, "Hi mom, I'm waving!"

In many ways, I find this the most difficult chapter to write. Living through the bodily and emotional difficulties I experienced while I was pregnant, writing those stories down and then re-living them over and over again during the writing of this book have been more tremendously challenging than I could have imagined. I am reminded by the words of Audre Lorde: "It is every woman's responsibility to live a considered life."[1] I remember Audre Lorde's contemplation of her life with breast cancer and I realize that, like her, I am sharply conscious of the fact that, through the writing of this book, I am not just considering my life, I am inviting others to also consider it. I am both looking at myself and showing/displaying myself. It is one thing to tell the story with my tongue, to speak it to other people, and yet another thing altogether to read the words I wrote during those difficult times. Speaking the story to another person is a public act where I have control over the delivery of the story and where I make constant decisions on how revealing to be. Reading the story in my journal is generally a private act where I am free to weep, to feel whatever it is that I need to feel. When I read my journal entries from my pregnancies, from the most difficult points in those lived experiences, sometimes a sentence will reach out and hit me so hard in the chest that I will physically buckle over and cry.

The deeper level of contemplation so necessary for writing about lived experiences often invokes intense personal reactions. The writing is an emotional process. Tears become full-out sobbing with my arms wrapped around myself in an effort to comfort, hold and protect me, this body and this spirit, from the startling reality of these words. At other times the mourning over what happened nauseates me and, in doubling over, my head comes so close to the keyboard that I cannot see the keys to the left or right of my nose, but it does not matter. Fingers, wet with splashing tears and shaky with excess emotion, keep putting down the memories, the thoughts, the feelings, the mourning, in words, one keystroke at a time. They have to come out. It has been through this experience of considering my life that I have learned that even a paraplegic can be "brought to her knees."

Like Audre Lorde, Arthur Frank also believes in the responsibility to consider one's life.[2] He argues that there is a powerful reciprocity that comes from the act of storytelling. Telling a story is important to the teller, but is also vital to the listener: "Telling stories in postmodern times, and perhaps in all times, attempts to change one's own life by affecting the lives of others."[3] In doing so, we acknowledge that the bodily experience continues where medicine leaves off. Frank believes that it is often hard to listen to stories of bodily suffering and that those voices are easy to ignore because they often remind others of our own vulnerabilities. Yet, despite how difficult it can be, he encourages us to listen, accept the faltering tone of the teller and be open to the ways in which the story can resonate with our own lives: "to realize the best potential in postmodern times requires an ethics of listening. I hope to show that in listening for the other, we listen for ourselves. The moment of witness in the story crystallizes a mutuality of need, when each is for the other."[4]

At the very same time, however, my pregnancy experiences were joyful and exciting. Those emotions appear in this text as well. To be reflective of the joy and of my personality, I have chosen to play with pregnancy euphemisms for the sub-titles in this chapter. Although I would normally opt for straightforwardness over colloquialisms, I chose to use these everyday and usually "taken for granted" terms to bring this chapter lightness and a sense of humour. I also hope that using these terms challenges readers to think about the words we use. After all, so many euphemisms are used to name bodily functions, body parts and sexual matters, as well as disabilities. Light and dark, bound together through this text, we will share my embodied experience with pregnancy.

Family Planning: How Shooting Gave Me Confidence

When I think back to all the negative social expectations that surrounded me, it was a wonder that I ever made the decision to become pregnant. When I think even more deeply, however, I know that my history with sport had a lot to do with my choice. Very simply, sport experiences gave me a certain, although surely a limited, confidence in my body's abilities. Some of this confidence was physical, a faith in my body to be able to be strong and perform as I trained it to. For example, after a training session in preparation for the 1992 Paralympics in Barcelona, I wrote:

July 26, 1992

I truly shine when I shoot well. My arm feels steady and strong, my heart rate is low and controlled, my breath is slow and in rhythm with my movements. Doing well gives me power and confidence. I know the competition will be tough in Barcelona, but sometimes I just feel that gold medal around my neck, the sun shining on my face and my Canadian flag raised for the world to see.

Some of this confidence was mental — I learned to choose my perspectives and how to reframe difficult situations. Some of my most meaningful experiences with confidence came from the adventures I had travelling to different places and leaving my comfort zone.

Memories of these experiences do not just live in my head; they also reside in certain everyday objects. For example, I recently found a Picasso print that had been stored away in our basement for a long time. Looking at it helped me remember a special time when I left my comfort zone. It was the Paralympics in Barcelona, Spain, in September 1992. I was twenty-three years old. My competitions were over and I had won a bronze medal in a category that had become much more challenging as it had been re-classified just prior to the games. The targets and the 10-ring had become smaller (for example, the very centre of an air rifle target — which one must hit in order to score a "10" — was now .5 millimetres, no bigger than the tip of a fine point pen). Another change to the competition was that there would be finals after the matches (a series of ten timed shots each added to the qualification round for the top eight competitors). The final consists of ten shots and the score zones are divided into decimals, so that each final shot may give up to 10.9 points. For example, instead of a shot being scored as a simple "10" or "9," shots would be additionally scored in degrees of 10 — a 10.1 would be a 10 that just cut the 10 ring, whereas a 10.9 would be a "perfect" 10. Because of the emphasis on absolute precision, the finals also add stress and pressure to competitors as well as a great deal of excitement for spectators. Moreover, due to the new classifications, I knew I would be competing against athletes with disabilities that were quite different (and some would say less disabling) than mine. As it turned out, I was the only wheelchair user on the podium; my other competitors could walk. I had shot well enough in the final to move from fourth place to third, thus earning my medal. I was feeling pretty good, strong and satisfied with my outcome. I wanted to treat myself by going to the Picasso Museum.

Neither my teammates nor my roommates were interested in going with me or had schedules that allowed them to take an afternoon off, so I decided to go alone. I felt excited, brave. I knew I would have to negotiate not just my own body, but also my wheelchair through cab rides, crusty cab drivers, Spanish language, a huge city, and a part of the city that had a reputation for being rough, dirty and a little dangerous.

I hailed a cab from just outside the village. The taxi was hot and sticky and so was I. I dismantled my chair for the driver, showing him how to do it, but I got the feeling that he was not interested in taking apart or putting together a wheelchair as long as I could do it myself. When I was dropped off at the admission desk of the museum, I remember feeling overwhelmingly hot, but as I entered the museum, I was struck by how deliciously cool it was in there, like I had just entered a very dignified and civilized place. My instincts told me I was in for a special time.

I remember feeling very independent, sophisticated and, at the age of twenty-three , very grown-up. I wore my red Canadian team uniform and felt proud of being a Canadian in this place. I took my time, making mental notes of how the artist's style had changed from his time in Paris to when he lived and worked in Spain. Without anyone to talk to about what I was seeing, I developed my own inner dialogue, which, from my sport psychology training, came easily and suited me just fine. I became particularly mesmerized watching how many times the theme of mother and child popped up in Picasso's paintings. On my way out of the museum, I picked up these three prints: the *Three Musicians*, a cubist painting that reflected my love of music, *The Embrace*, which was lovely and romantic, and *Maternidad*, an image of a mother protectively holding a small child.

Clearly, my feelings of confidence went beyond performing well athletically and winning medals. This is reflected in my journal.

September 10, 1992

> Going to the museum alone was a rush. I felt like I was on a real adventure, that I was a strong and independent woman in charge. It wasn't just going to the museum; I am talking about the choice to make a bold decision, to carry that decision out, and to feel good while doing it. Being in Barcelona (and winning the medal and making the 3P final), I feel like I am able to take on whatever challenge that I choose.

Getting the prints back to Canada in one piece was no easy task. On the way back to the village, I once again had to negotiate my body and wheelchair, as well as these precious rolled up prints, into and out of a taxi in a huge, hot and humid city. I packed the prints in bubble wrap and tucked them in my equipment bag amongst my leather shooting jacket, aluminum shooting table, and other "less than soft" sports items. I gave the prints a kiss and hoped for the best. When they arrived home in almost perfect condition, I had them framed.

I was particularly attached to the *Maternidad* print. I remember when my roommate asked me why I chose this particular one when there were so many to choose from, I replied, "it was the one that haunted me." When I look at this framed print now, I believe it was not a coincidence that led me to choose it. Although I was not admitting it out loud, I secretly yearned to experience the love of a child. As I read the above story, I am also struck by how I chose to navigate my body through that journey to the museum, and how in many (probably unconscious) ways I was preparing myself for the intense and demanding challenge of becoming a mother. I was okay with my physical life being difficult and I was becoming accustomed to having the confidence necessary to take risks. I am convinced that my involvement with sport is what gave me this confidence.

It is important to address here the influence that Finn was having on me during my competitive years. Even though he has not coached me for over fifteen years now, I still feel strongly attached to him. He had a gift for adjusting his coaching style to different personalities thereby making each of his athletes feel connected to him. He seemed to understand a potential that was within me and he was comfortable with regularly articulating that to me. He would say, "You exude confidence" and "You were born to succeed" when I least expected him to. Aware of how I was a young girl compared to many of my shooting peers, he would also talk about me in only the most positive of terms around our team as well as when we collaborated with other national teams, such as the year we worked with the U.S. team at the Colorado Springs Olympic Training Centre. While my teammates would jokingly (and lovingly) disparage me for being a girl, I do not recall that Finn ever did, not even once. I also remember one time in particular when he told some American shooters: "Heather has forgotten more about shooting than most shooters ever get to know." Comments like this, coupled with his strong Danish accent, made him an endearing and loveable character to shooters all over the world, and his confidence in me eventually became my own. In other words, I began to believe him. I developed a confidence within myself and I became stronger, more self-assured and eventually a leader and, later, a coach in my athletic community.

Finn also respected my need to keep notes and journals. He always declared that writing was not his strong point and that he disliked paperwork, and yet, he took the time at a training camp on September 25, 1988, just prior to the Paralympics in Seoul, Korea, to write me a poem. Because it is meaningful to me beyond shooting, I have kept this poem in a safe place and I refer to it whenever I need to smile or remember reasons I can be bold and that I should have faith in myself.

Heather be bold
In that rifle barrel lies gold
It could happen in four years
If not to my eyes it will bring tears
Don't let it mold
Nor get too old
Heather be bold
— Your Coach.

Another great gift I received from Finn was how to treat situations positively — he would often tell me: "If worrying is going to help your situation, then worry like hell." I do not remember him ever becoming angry with any of his athletes and, as I recall, there were many times when anger would have been understandable. Likewise, he did not complain when the conditions were less than perfect; he saw those circumstances as opportunities for all of us to "get comfortable with being uncomfortable." It was perhaps this "re-framing" that I gained the most from — understanding the power of being able to choose my perspective, my viewpoint on any given situation.

Upon Finn's retirement, I wrote in my journal:

September 27, 1994

My whole life drastically changed when I ended up on the national team and going to California for the World Championship. I learned independence, a different kind of strength that comes from being out of one's "comfort zone," and I developed a new sense of self — someone I did not even know existed. The competition was good for me, the mental training was too. But the best part was the people I became so close to and learned so much from. This team was my other family, my community. Finn described the feeling of family among this team as being like the first time you fall in love, and how that cannot be duplicated.

And Finn, I do not know who I would be without him. He taught me how to have confidence in myself and why I should have confidence in myself. He taught me how to see everything and anything in the way that I decide I want to see it. I could reframe any situation then... and I owe all that to him.

I do not think that either Finn or I could have predicted how this skill would help me through my pregnancies. However, during these times, I often used the tools of re-framing to manage difficult situations as well as my sometimes overwhelming emotions.

February 24, 1997

I am not complaining, just stating the facts. And the facts are also that this pregnancy has been hard, probably the hardest thing I have ever done, both physically and emotionally. I have to believe that hard isn't necessarily bad, and easy isn't necessarily good. I hope that someday I will be able to look at this time with wonder and appreciation and say "wow, look at all I have learned."

Knocked Up and Knocked Out: Autonomic Dysreflexia

The first such difficult circumstance was in the first trimester with my first pregnancy. It was emotionally challenging and physically difficult because I suffered an acute attack of autonomic dysreflexia due to a urinary tract infection that quickly spread to my kidneys and bloodstream, making me septic. Autonomic dysreflexia (AD) is a potentially life-threatening condition that occurs in spinal cord injured persons with lesions on T6 and below.[5] It is triggered by painful or noxious stimuli such as a bladder infection, a bone fracture or any kind of wound and can result in high blood pressure, pounding headaches and sweating. Complications can result in seizures, pulmonary edema, myocardial infarction or cerebral haemorrhage, stroke and death. In my journal I wrote:

October 6, 1996

This baby must really want to be here. She/he has been through a nightmare in the last few days.

Last Tuesday I suspected a urinary tract infection. I took a sample to the Dr's office, but because the results were not in on Thursday, I did not get any antibiotics. Thursday night I became very ill. It started with severe chills for a few hours and then a raging fever. Darrell and I figured it must be dysreflexia which can happen to people with scɪ's at T6 levels or higher. I knew my blood pressure was high because my head was pulsing so hard with each of my heartbeats. I really wondered if I would die. I don't know that I would have made the night if Darrell had not been there. Dr. S. had sent us some information on autonomic dysreflexia a while back so Darrell dug that out of my briefcase and read what to do. The first thing he saw was "This Emergency can be Fatal" in bold letters at the top. He wanted to take me to Emergency, due to the second bout of chills and fever I had, but of course I wouldn't go, I couldn't go. I couldn't get out of bed. And he wanted to call an ambulance, but I didn't want that either. I wanted to just give it a little time. So we did. Darrell sat me up, as he read he should do, helped me to the bathroom so I could empty my bladder. All of it eventually worked well enough and I settled around 3 a.m. It was much harder for Darrell than for me,

> without a doubt. I was also quite disoriented and it really scared him. I am sorry for that. But I am grateful he was there, nevertheless.
>
> In the morning we went in to Emergency. The resident on call wanted to admit me, but because I was feeling better, I talked him out of it. They did blood work though, a special test where they take blood from both arms. I went home and had a good sleep. At 7 a.m. the resident called and said my blood culture was positive, meaning that the infection had travelled into my bloodstream. So here I am, in room 3031, and will be here for a while, apparently.
>
> The Dr. says that the baby should be fine. We will have an ultrasound tomorrow: my birthday. I hope Darrell will be able to come.
>
> So far this stay in the hospital has pretty well been awful. Although the IV went in well yesterday, I had a high fever and chills again and generally felt horrible. Today the IV had to come out and it took 5 tries to get another line. Dr. H. from Anesthesiology was the last resort and she found a vein and made it work right away. They had been collectively trying for over an hour so when Dr. H found it so quickly, I was so relieved and grateful. All the trying had been torture. My veins are fairly prominent, but they are thick with scar tissue and very hard to penetrate, and keep, a needle. I have blue and purple bruises up and down both my arms. The new IV is in my left hand.
>
> The whole IV ordeal was very upsetting for me and I have been crying a lot. I pray the IV stays in this time. I am terrified of being dug into again. I can't do it alone anymore, I can't, I swear. Please, God, I am not kidding, just a small amount of mercy, please.

My episode with AD was frightening. However, I responded well to a course of intravenous antibiotics and a prophylactic antibiotic for the duration of my pregnancy. I could have possibly prevented this episode with AD from happening if I had just had access to more information about how a body with a spinal cord injury sometimes experiences pregnancy.

With Child: Seeing Is Believing with Ultrasounds

It was after this episode with AD that my doctor insisted on having regularly scheduled ultrasounds so that we could closely watch the growth of the baby. Based on that history, it was decided we should do the same for my second pregnancy. Although I was happy to have the ultrasounds done, I still yearned to know more about how my spinal cord injury would affect the rest of my pregnancy and the birthing process. It made sense to me that if I could at least know more about the baby, I would have a bit more control over what was happening to my body. For example, although having ultrasounds done was physically difficult for me, I also loved seeing my babies.

January 30, 1997

I had a rough night again. I have to do my glucose tolerance test today. I also had another ultrasound which was also hard on me. Filling my bladder so full makes my legs even more spastic than usual and because they need to be straight out in front of me while I lay on my back, it is very uncomfortable and exhausting. Darrell holds them and straightens them the best that he can. However, what is important is that all looks good on the inside. Pat is now four pounds, six ounces and has a heart rate of 142 bpm which is good. He is lying in a good position, head down, feet up, spine to the right.

May 3, 2005

Well, I have my facts. Our first six-week ultrasound is complete and we have seen a teeny heartbeat. I wish ultrasounds were not so hard. It is necessary to fill my bladder so that the ultrasound can see my uterus but it is an extremely uncomfortable procedure. Filling, but not draining my bladder brings on autonomic dysreflexia and is something I wouldn't wish on anyone. It makes my legs spasm hard which makes it difficult for the technician to get the information that she needed. I feel bad about that but at the same time my head is pounding, I am sweating, and I am caught in the conflict of wanting to focus on the beauty of this moment of seeing my baby for the first time and wishing it could all be over as soon as possible.

Darrell held my legs down as best he could. To add further embarrassment to this already awkward situation, my bladder burst and leaked on to my pants and the examination table. I had to go home and change my pants as well as my shirt, which was soaked with sweat.

Feeling bad about the spasms and reaction of autonomic dysreflexia that made my ultrasound technician's job more difficult was part of my anxiety over public scrutiny of my pregnancy. According to Rosalyn Diprose, my feelings were justified. She argues that the pregnant body is the target of surveillance and that a social network of surveillance practices are in place in order to continuously monitor mothers and parenting methods. Pregnant women are judged on what they eat, how they move, how "big" they get and the decisions they make about work, rest, exercise and even dress. [6] While most of these concerns are undoubtedly based in genuine concern for overall health and wellness, there is also an underlying message at play about what constitutes a competent and healthy mothering body. The power of these messages and practices is that we generally do not even realize they are occurring. The fact that I was pregnant and had a disability only served to accentuate this scrutiny. I felt like I was being watched and evaluated, especially in public places like the mall or the grocery store. I felt like I did not get the approving smiles from strangers, like I heard that other pregnant women did. When I was with Darrell, however, I felt that the glances were more "approving," as though I needed his presence to secure my social collateral, or to provide at least part of an answer to the puzzle of being a pregnant woman in a wheelchair.

Furthermore, women may desire the monitoring of their reproductive bodies by attending to the message that these surveillance practices help them feel in control and knowledgeable about their pregnancies.[7] I know I certainly valued the feelings of control and knowledge that ultrasounds seemed to give me and with knowing so little about how my body could handle pregnancy, I devoured any information I could get despite the pain and discomfort my body felt while having the ultrasounds done.

I had experienced a life-long history with often being seen as weak and helpless. Once I was pregnant, I strongly desired to be seen as strong and in control more than I probably ever had before. Women and people with disabilities often represent dependency, vulnerability and weakness, and Michel Foucault argues that bodies such as these represent what he terms "docile bodies."[8] Docile bodies are ones that are regulated through a set of regimented disciplinary acts. From cosmetic surgery to fashion trends, there are many ways in which social forces try to normalize "deviant" bodies, or bodies that are not white, privileged, able or heterosexual, into docile bodies. In his book *Discipline and Punish*, Michel Foucault looks at the practices of disciplinary power through settings such as prisons, hospitals, factories and schools but, according to Shelley Tremain, who writes about Michel Foucault through a disability lens, the ideas can also be used more extensively when understanding social regulation and control in areas concerned with disabilities such as asylums, workers' compensation benefits, special education, sheltered workshops, telethons and pre-natal diagnosis.[9] By creating and maintaining these systems and institutions, we attempt to reinforce cultural norms that conform to acceptable ideas of gender, race, sex, class and ability. When I reflect on and question disciplinary techniques, for example, why I had the ultrasounds done, I think of two things: One, I wanted to "see" my baby and therefore know more about him or her. I did this in the spirit of Judith Butler's ideas on "performativity," an idea that during gender development one acts in a way that is considered male or female, and those acts are reinforced by social norms.[10] Gender, for Judith Butler, is an action, a "performance," rather than a fixed concept. These ideas on performativity make sense to me now as I reflect on how much I wanted to "do" pregnancy like other women do. Ultrasounds are part of a "normal" pregnant woman's experience. Secondly, and ultimately, however, I had ultrasounds done because my doctor ordered them. In this light, essentially everyone perpetuates the idea of the docile body, and I feel that mine was simply a more highly watched docile body.

In many ways, mine was an atypical docile body existing outside the boundaries of the experience, expectation or understanding of those that held sway over my physical presence at many points during my pregnancies.

> February 12, 1997
>
> Because this is an experience my body was never expected to have, I am having a lot of challenges integrating these new ideas into my sense of self. I have so little information about how this pregnancy is supposed to be for my kind of body, if I could just have a little control, a little information about the baby, I think I would feel more secure. Knowing the sex would just be ONE thing I actually know about this pregnancy. I don't think anyone gets it.

During my first pregnancy in particular, many ultrasounds were scheduled for me and because it was so important for me to know as much as I could about my pregnancy, I had a strong desire to know the sex of my unborn child. I saw the many ultrasounds as many opportunities to see the sex, but I was terribly disappointed when my ultrasound technician refused to pass this knowledge on to our doctor, and therefore on to us. Our conversation about this quickly went from a discussion about knowing a baby's sex to an argument about disability. Our conflict went like this:

> Me: If you are able to tell, I want to know the sex of this baby.
>
> C: That is not important to know, Heather.
>
> Me: Why?
>
> C: Parents only want to know for entertainment purposes. They just want to know how to decorate the nursery or what colour clothes to buy.
>
> Me: That has nothing to do with it for us. If the baby is a boy he can wear pink! Seriously, I need information to help me adjust mentally. This pregnancy has been a lot for me to take in and there is not much information about what I can expect.
>
> C: All that matters is whether or not the baby is healthy.
>
> Me: What if the baby is not this so-called healthy?
>
> C: Then mom and dad have choices.
>
> Me: (Hotly) Not in my house they don't. Whether or not the baby has a disability is irrelevant to me. I will still want this baby! (C went about her business, ignoring my argument).

I turned to Darrell and whispered to him I did not want to call the baby an "it" anymore. He sighed heavily as these on-going ethical conversations with C were beginning to wear on him. He knew she had no intention of letting us know the sex of our baby so he smiled and said in a voice only I could hear: "We are probably not going to know. It is okay. Let's just call the baby Pat." He was referring to the androgynous character, "Pat," played by Julia Sweeny on *Saturday Night Live* who always had viewers guessing whether she/he was male/female. Despite my frustration with C, I laughed out loud and agreed. The baby was "Pat" to us until he was born and we named him Patrick.

What is not a laughing matter, however, were the messages I received about the lack of value and appreciation we have for disabilities and diversity. Rosemarie Garland-Thomson asserts, "The popular utopian belief that all forms of disability can be eliminated through prophylactic manipulation of genetics will only serve to intensify the prejudice against those who inevitably will acquire disabilities through aging and encounters with the environment."[11] Susan Wendell agrees, "To people who value disabilities as differences, attempts to prevent disability by preventing the birth of people with disabilities can seem analogous to attempts to guarantee the birth of male babies because they are more highly valued, or to wipe out colour differences by genetic technologies."[12] I believe my ultrasound experiences were larger social, political and bioethical issues concerning the lack of worth we have for disabilities and how we want to avoid them at all costs. Susan Wendell bluntly asks, "Is saying 'Everyone wants a healthy baby,' morally and politically similar to saying, 'Everyone wants a white baby?' If not, how is it different?"[13] Furthermore, I question what the definition of "healthy" is.

Feminists have historically justified a woman's power to choose by giving the example of the disabled fetus as a reason why a woman should be able to have an abortion.[14] While I would not argue with a woman's right to choose what happens with her body, I do object to the argument that it is justifiable to abort a fetus just because a disability may be involved. I know that it was this personal belief that fueled my frustration with not knowing the sex of my own baby during my first pregnancy and why my husband and I opted to not test for different disabilities while I was pregnant the second time. Susan Wendell sums it up best for me: "People who take it for granted that it would be a good thing to wipe out all biological causes of disability (as opposed to social causes) are far more confident that they know how to perfect nature and humanity than I am."[15]

There Is No Recipe for This Bun in the Oven: Lack of Information

Although research on women's embodied experiences and pregnancy has been embraced by feminist scholars,[16] feminist research has largely ignored the bodily issues, including pregnancy, of women with disabilities.[17] For women with disabilities, the expectations tend toward not taking on adult social roles such as wife, partner, lover or mother.[18] As a result, discourse on motherhood and that of disability rarely occur in combination.[19]

> March 9, 1997
>
> Dear Sharon,
>
> Our public health nurse was here to discuss labour, delivery, etc. with us. It is not likely that I will need to get any instruction on breathing, labour pain management, etc. since I don't have functioning abdominal muscles and therefore I won't be able to push. The nurse also came over last week to go over breastfeeding. Sometimes I know more about what I need than she does, in respect to my paralysis that is. So we end up learning a lot from each other. She's very nice, but she asked if I will have a c-section. I think I might scream if someone else asks me if I will have to have a c-section. I mean, maybe I will, it is a possibility for any woman, but why is it always assumed for my body? My vagina worked well enough to get pregnant in the first place, didn't it?
>
> Love, Heather

A mother is traditionally seen as an adult who is physically able and therefore sexually capable. For most people, this typification does not apply to women with disabilities.[20] Some argue that a woman with a disability even seems to pose a danger to society: "Society generally invalidates disabled women's sexuality. If anything, our reproductive potential is feared. We are presumed either incapable of producing the kind of babies society wants — healthy babies — or incapable of adequately nurturing children."[21] Disability theorists Michelle Fine and Adrienne Asch argue: "Motherhood, the institution and experience that perhaps dominated all cultural conceptions of women — eclipsing even expectations of beauty, softness, or ever-present sexuality — often has been proscribed for a woman with a disability."[22] There was so little information on how women with spinal cord injuries can experience pregnancy that I simply had to deal with one challenge after the other with the limited resources I had.

January 12, 1997

I don't want to go back to work tomorrow. Last week was hard on me due to a lot of back pain and increased spasticity in my legs. I have also been dizzy and light headed, which is scary. I really do not know what is going on, but I know I had better take a leave of absence soon, for Pat's sake as well as my own.

January 13, 1997

While at work today, I fainted in the bathroom. With some help, I called Dr. T's office, spoke to the nurse, who told me to come in as soon as possible so that she could check my blood pressure. By the time I got there, I was feeling a bit better, but Dr. T suspects what happened was due to Pat's pressure on my spine, so I feel faint because I am not getting enough blood to my brain in those moments. He feels my restricted blood flow would not be as much of an issue if I could stand up, walk, and stretch. If these episodes increase, I will need to be on bed rest.

February 17, 1997

I am coughing up stuff which makes me worry that I have an infection. I am scared that I am going to end up in the hospital again. I saw Dr. C today though and she reassured me that Pat is okay and well protected.

Thank God I am not at work or it would be much harder to manage this. It is not like I am on vacation though. It is hard just getting through each day. My pain and fatigue are difficult enough, but transfers in and out of my chair have gotten harder too. I try to minimize how many times I get in and out and I am not having regular showers or baths anymore. I should be drinking more to help get rid of this cold, but that means I will have to do more transfers in the bathroom.

During this time of great physical change with so little information about what I could expect, it only took one small positive comment from my doctor's resident to give me some feelings of confidence and support.

February 27, 1997

This has been a long, full day. We began with our Dr.'s appointment this morning. Dr. B found Pat lying sideways again. She thinks this is partly due to a lack of gravity to pull Pat in the right direction since I don't stand or walk. I told her that I think when I am sitting, Pat has more room and probably more comfort when he lies sideways. I sure feel more comfortable, less crowded and like I can breathe easier. Pat's heart rate is 130 bpm. Next time will be our last ultrasound and all the measurements will be taken. We may have a cervix exam done then too. After that, we will go in every week to see the Dr. until Pat is born. Dr. B said she was just remarking to Dr. T about how well I am doing and that made me feel great. I don't hear that kind of thing very often. Everyone else tends to focus on my problems and my disability.

When I now think about Dr. B's positive comment, I agree with her. I was doing really well with my pregnancy. I was active, eating well and adjusting to an identity I had not imagined for myself. I was managing a job, the negative reactions of others and the necessary adaptations to our home. I also see that I should have been giving myself more credit and that I deserved more credit for how well I was doing from others. When I reflect on why her comment was so memorable, it was because the sentiment was out of step with the traditionally held beliefs about women with disabilities as dependent, weak and vulnerable and not as autonomous and robust. Dr. B's words reflected that I was strong and capable; these were opinions I was not accustomed to hearing, and I was grateful to her.

Eating but Not Medicating for Two

Part of feeling strong and in control of my mind and body has also been my diligent decision-making about taking medications. Even as a child, I have been critical of the number and amount of medications that have been prescribed to me. However, to control the spasms in my lower extremities, I find Baclophen, commonly prescribed for people with spinal cord injuries, truly helpful. When I found out I was pregnant with my second baby, I was advised by my doctor to stop ingesting it, at least for the first trimester. I readily agreed because I did not want to do anything that might harm my baby. Omitting it, however, had more of an effect than just increased spasms. I also had a lot of difficulty falling asleep and getting recuperative sleep. The lack of sleep and living with a body that was never still was hard on me psychologically and only contributed to my already overly emotional state of mind.

May 24, 2005

I am now nine weeks pregnant. The hardest physical part has been the absence of most of my medications, especially Baclophen which helps settle my legs and allows me to sleep. However, when I don't sleep, opportunities remain to learn about my body. I used to sleep through some of my pain, discomfort and spasms. Now I cannot sleep through them, but I seem to understand where the spasms are coming from. The problem seems to be in my right leg and in my back. Lying on my right side is impossible and since this is the only position where I have been able to sleep in for years, obviously I am not sleeping. I wish I could sleep sitting up. Lying down seems to aggravate the pain and spasms.

The lack of sleep and the hormonal changes have made me emotional. The pulling and spasms in my abdomen that stem from my back pain is so uncomfortable. It is hard to breathe. My digestion is also out of whack. I am either constipated or I have diarrhea. I was rarely at ease with my body before, but now I am feeling like it is unrecognizable — a complete stranger. I am trying to honour it by feeding it well and keeping it active. I see Patrick at lunch and I pick him up from school. I walk our dog Bailey every day.

What Not to Expect When You Are Expecting

April 20, 2005

Everywhere I look, I see babies. There were babies in the restaurant too. However, I do not see any families where the mom is using a wheelchair.

There are many ways in which my experience with pregnancy appeared to be similar to the way other women would experience pregnancy. I believed that at least part of my pregnancy would be "normal" and in an effort to find my experience reflected in the world outside of me I read *What to Expect When You Are Expecting* and *The Girlfriend's Guide to Pregnancy* (books that are considered pregnancy "bibles") as well as countless pregnancy magazines. I also subscribed to a group on the Internet that sent me week-by-week details of how my baby was developing and what to expect from the "average" pregnant body. I followed the latest nutritional advice and watched for and celebrated the signs of what the texts consistently called a "normal and healthy" pregnancy.

September 12, 1996

So much has happened to my body that has not happened to most people. Now I am pregnant which is something that happens to many women. This is the most bizarre, yet normal phenomenon I have ever experienced.

December 6, 1996

I think Pat kicked me for the first time! It took my body by surprise. My legs went out straight in front of me in spasm and my torso was thrown back in my chair. I didn't really feel anything on the inside, but I saw what happened to my body from the outside. I hope it happens again soon. I want to be sure.

December 19, 1996

I felt Pat kick me today, from the outside of my belly. It happened this morning while I was lying in bed talking to Darrell. I have had feeling of movement before but I was never 100% sure that it was Pat. I thought it might be a spasm and I was afraid to admit the kick, in case it wasn't real. But today, I know that kick was real, my hands absolutely felt kicking. In fact, Pat booted me about 12 times, and Darrell felt it too so I have a witness. He says that in many ways, I am the first woman to have a baby.

However, I sometimes found myself wishing that I knew someone else who had experienced pregnancy while living with a spinal cord injury. I missed my peers with disabilities that I had become connected to through sport because of the disability-related issues I was facing during pregnancy. Gill calls this part of disability identity development as "coming home."[23] Coming home illustrates the level of connection, ease and comfort that people with disabilities have with other people with disabilities and who share their disability issues. At the same time, however, I knew that even if I could connect with my teammates, their ability to empathize would be limited because they were all men.

February 9, 1997

My digestion and elimination processes have always been a tremendous source of shame because I have so little control over the process, and now I have less control that ever before. The only people who understand are my buddies in wheelchairs but they are all men and they don't know anything about being pregnant. And besides, they all live so far away.

February 20, 1997

M, the nurse from Public Health came to talk to us about breastfeeding this morning. I just want to do it. I want to do it for Pat's sake. My only two concerns are that my injury is right at nipple level, so I don't know if that will affect my milk supply. I am also concerned about not having support if things go poorly. My mom and Darrell's mom did not breastfeed.

Not only did I not have other moms with disabilities to accompany me in my pregnancy and childbirth journey, I must repeat here that I did not have enough information about what I could expect from my own body. With a lack of resources at my disposal, I did not know how my body would adapt to pregnancy, childbirth or breastfeeding. Although I was taking care of myself and my developing baby the best I could with the information I did have, I still had underlying fears that my body was not truly capable of pregnancy and giving birth.

March 15, 1997

Tonight I hope I can sleep without having any bad dreams. I have had a
few nights of scary dreams about Pat, Darrell, and I. Last night I dreamt
about the Children's Rehab Centre in vivid detail. The night before
I dreamt that I gave birth, but only to a lot of fluid and a cord — no
baby. I asked Darrell if he thought a person can know something is real
intellectually, but not know it in her heart. He says he thinks I am normal,
that these fears and feelings and denial are normal. Little Pat, I know that
I need you. I need to see your face and touch you — and soon. I feel
more ready for you now than ever before. Please come soon.

Additionally, my doctors had a limited understanding of how my body
would be affected by pregnancy and childbirth. The many unknowns and
uncertainties during my pregnancy often left me feeling vulnerable and
frightened. Women with disabilities may experience complexities with their
health issues that medical services need to adapt to.[24] Gill also asserts that in
addition to other women's health issues such as osteoporosis and disability,
more research is needed about reproduction health, hormone functioning,
fertility, contraception and parenting in women with disabilities. Furthermore,
others have stated how some women with spinal cord injuries have suffered
because of the way contractions caused dysreflexia, which brought on high
blood pressure, strokes and even death.[25]

January 30, 1997

I have been up since 5 a.m. My back hurts so much and I can only sleep
in one position, which is my right side which is aching. I have too much
of a belly to lie on my back — restricted blood flow to my head I've
been told. And I can't lie on my left side because of my dislocated hip.
All the books say to lie on your left, it is best for the baby. I guess most
pregnant women don't have dislocated hips. I also have a headache and
I am congested. I have tried all kinds of things to relax — writing in here
is my last resort. Writing in here is what keeps me focused and strong
and relatively positive.

February 3, 1997

I fluctuate between good and bad days and on the good, I just try to
keep busy. When they are bad, they are just bad and it is all I can do
to not just sit around feeling sorry for myself! When I sit too long or in
the wrong position, I get violent abdominal spasms and I am unable to
sit up. It is quite uncomfortable and a little scary because I don't know
what is going on. The transfers in and out of my chair are hard now,

> mostly because my legs don't want to cooperate. Pat seems to be fine
> though. He has a strong heart rate, he also kicks, moves, and wiggles a lot.
>
> March 22, 1997
>
> Our last Dr. appointment scared me. Pat is in the right direction but
> hasn't yet dropped. If Pat does not drop by our appointment next week,
> we may have to seriously consider a c-section delivery. And if my water
> breaks, Pat's head won't act as a "cork" and that could be dangerous
> because the cord might come down. This is also a risk of my membranes
> rupturing. These things may not be detected by me because I can't feel
> much. This is not good if they happen and then I would need to get to
> the hospital right away.
>
> The thought of something happening to Pat is very upsetting. It is
> as though a great wave of protective feelings have overwhelmed me. I
> am trying to think positively and have faith that everything is going to
> be okay.

Whereas maternal mortality is now a phenomenon that rarely occurs, pregnancy and childbirth can certainly increase complicating factors for women with permanent disabilities or chronic illnesses.[26] Health care providers simply do not know enough about the intersection of pregnancy, childbirth and disability.[27] Even obstetricians who specialize in high-risk pregnancies lack this kind of information and their priority tends to be on the health of the fetus.[28] This certainly resonates with my second experience with pregnancy. My doctor was open about his lack of interest in how my paraplegic body was being affected during pregnancy. He did not want to understand or deal with my spinal cord injury. Any issues related to my paralysis were always passed off to my rehabilitation medicine doctor.

Riding the Baby Train Alone: Without Community

My feelings about a lack of community continued into my second pregnancy. As a result, I would get frustrated and even angry with messages, whether through media or from people, about how "all" women experience pregnancy. I think I wanted someone to acknowledge that what I was experiencing was different, a feeling that was escalated probably because my experience was also physically and emotionally difficult. Without a community to see my experiences reflected in, I often felt lonely and scared. It was not just the absence of pregnant women in wheelchairs, it was the ubiquitous presence of non-disabled pregnancy images — women that were walking and "healthy" and wearing their pregnancies like fashion statements. There were images of the fit, active, sexy pregnant woman on the covers of fashion magazines, on magazines entirely devoted to pregnancy and childbirth and on daily television shows (on networks such as TLC and Slice). "Healthy" pregnancy and childbirth books warrant an entire section of our large local bookstore. Since I could not fit that image in many if not most ways, I had several moments of bitterness laced with humour and sarcasm. It was a way of coping.

Sometimes with all the difficulties we were experiencing, Darrell and I just needed to laugh. It has been my experience that "crip humour" or "in-group humour" is often used by people with disabilities to identify, challenge and simply deal with the barriers — both architectural and attitudinal — that exist in our everyday lives.[29] Humour can give people with disabilities the permission to be angry and frustrated.

> February 26, 1997
>
> I am growing weary of all the people who ask if I will automatically have to have a cesarean section. Darrell is a little tired of this assumption too, so he has taken the approach of telling people that while we are not so worried about how a vaginal birth will go for me, we are concerned about how the baby's little wheelchair will come out. This shocks people, most of the time they laugh, and hopefully they get the message that my body was capable of making this baby, therefore, it is capable of delivering it too. He says he wants them to see that while my disability is certainly important in this pregnancy; my body is also more than my disability.

Although I certainly had light and funny moments like this during my second pregnancy, my journal's angry moments stood out even more.

> April 22, 2005
>
> I am waiting to have my blood work done after having just finished a complicated procedure of giving a urine sample. Fill to the line of the first container then fill the second to the top. I have heard many women complain about this, claiming the task is hard to do. I want to say to them, "Do this with one hand and a catheter! Then do this when your bladder is totally full, you are having dysreflexia, and your legs are spasming. Talk to me about how hard it is then." I may be sensitive right now, but the women in the clinic seemed annoyed at the length of time I spent in the bathroom. Argh!

> November 15, 2005
>
> I hate "The Mom Show." These women are rich, white, spoiled, superficial, boring, and without any real problems. I want to like it, some of the information is good, but I simply can't relate to these pretty, perfect, coifed women.
>
> Furthermore, if I see one more poster, or segment in a book, or

column in a magazine telling me how great Kegel exercises are and how and why I need to do them, I will scream, cry, and rip up the very paper I see it on. Watch out, Doctor's office, I am ready to do some vandalism.

November 26, 2005

Why did I have to get this cold on top of everything else? With a cough that keeps me awake at night and is sometimes so harsh I will gag and vomit? And a pressure sore? And severe sweats that no one understands how uncomfortable they make me, and constipation in addition to zero bladder control? The nurse says lots of women develop a lack of bladder control and I am no different. But that is bullshit. I am different. These women can get up, get easily cleaned up, do not have to do loads and loads of laundry including cushion covers, sheets, bed protectors, towels, underwear, pants, socks, even shirts. These things make my situation with bladder control very different indeed. I still haven't gotten the smell out of my cushion's foam part completely, or out of my chair's upholstery. Do other women have this problem? Do other women have rods in their backs that are broken and out of place and in need of major surgery? Not fucking likely.

A woman at Pat's school commented to me yesterday about how I will be giving up sleeping through the night. Without thinking, I told her that I haven't had a full night's sleep for months. "Just can't get comfortable?" she asked, and without waiting for an answer, she proceeded to go on about how she couldn't get comfortable in her last few weeks. I just didn't need to hear it. People have no idea. It's not their fault, how could they know? But I still want them to shut the fuck up. I want someone to inhabit my body, for a day, even a few hours, to experience this, to feel what I feel, in order to make myself heard, to validate my experience. No matter how much Darrell and Patrick love and support me, I still feel so very much alone.

When I think back to this time, I am reminded of how, although I may have sometimes felt alone, I also had the support of many people who love me, like my mom and dad, my parents-in-law, my brothers and sister, their spouses and their families, and my friends. My friends offered some of the most meaningful encouragement — the smallest of positive comments made a significant difference in how I coped. A friend and former co-worker, Jana, who is also a mother of three boys and who knows well how pregnancy is measured in weeks, called me on the telephone to congratulate me on "surviving and thriving" through another week; Eileen spontaneously sent me flowers; Cory made me borscht with the beets he grew in his garden; Jody helped me to my doctor's appointments when Darrell could not. Many people took care of us in many ways.

> *We have everything we need*
> *And I will care for you*
> *'Cause you care for me*
> *(Xavier Rudd, "Better People")*

I took comfort in music. Patrick would play the guitar for me, I would listen to the songs that I loved to sing, songs of hope and promises kept, and of how love matters more than anything.

I also had my "mental game" that I had learned from sport. Through the pain, the sweat and my constantly spastic legs, I would go deep inside myself, listen to my heart beat, focus on my breath and say over and over again, "all my cells are strong. All six trillion of my cells are strong, healthy and well."

And of course, I had Darrell. I would tenderly and carefully lie down in our bed at the end of each day and I would ask him the same thing, "how am I doing this?" He would take my hand, and reply, "with me, with strength, with love. Hold on." And so I did.

> *We went travelling on the road*
> *I noticed there were stones along the way*
> *I bent to move the boulders from the road*
> *You said "it's best to leave those pebbles where they lay"*
> *And then I saw the patience in your smile*
> *and hand in hand we danced as the miles passed by*
> *(Eileen Laverty, "The Road")*

On Stork Watch: My Body Matters Now

At the same time as I was feeling displaced, lonely and sometimes angry, I also had many other times when I felt more validated as a woman while I was pregnant than I ever had before. My pregnancies enabled me to feel truly "female" because I was experiencing something that many women also experience and because of how my body was changing into ways that felt feminine to me. I also felt like my body "mattered" in ways it never did before. In other words, I felt as though my body was "showing" more societal worth than it did when I was not pregnant. I also often felt a strong sense of positive femininity and a brand new sense of sexuality.

December 8, 1996

Dear Sharon,

Buying groceries last night, we saw your dad. He says Deb, your sister-in-law, looks enormous and is due in February. I smiled at that. I feel enormous too. I am round and ripe. My belly is so pronounced, my breasts are bigger, and a lot of people say I have "the glow" of pregnancy. My body image has never been worse. Or better. I belong to a group now, a special club called "woman" in ways I never dreamed I ever would.

Love, Heather

Once my pregnancies were over and my children were born, I found myself remarking to friends and family how I still wished I was pregnant. I remember telling my thesis supervisor, Dr. Donna Goodwin, that I loved being pregnant, that the experience made me feel "special." When I reflect on that now, however, I realize that pregnancy did not make me feel special, rather the experience made me feel normal. When pregnant, I was often not the "Other" for probably the first time in my life.

There Is Nothing Delicate about This Condition: Strength and Power from Belonging

The theory of Otherness is a useful concept in understanding people with disabilities. Feminist writer Simone de Beauvoir coined the terms "Self" and "Other" to illuminate how men are considered essential and women are created inessential; man is the subject, woman is the other.[30] Susan Wendell has further insights:

> When we make people 'Other,' we group them together as the objects of our experience instead of seeing them primarily as symbolic of something else — usually, but not always, something we reject and fear and project onto them. To the non-disabled, people with disabilities and people with dangerous or incurable illnesses symbolize, among other things, imperfection, failure to control the body, and everyone's vulnerability to weakness, pain, and death.[31]

One day while I waited to see my doctor at the rehabilitation unit, I noticed some of the other wheelchair users in the waiting area. I scrawled many words in tiny script in the margins alongside the passage in Susan Wendell's book:

> Even more than winning Paralympic medals and demonstrating physical competence through athleticism, pregnancy and breastfeeding flies in the face of the notion of being the Other. For the first time in my life I had feelings of femaleness and belonging. These feelings, whether they are right or wrong, made me feel more normal. It was like, "See? I am not so different. I can do what other women do — my body is sexual, strong, and healthy — this baby proves it!"

Later on, as my wait for the doctor's appointment dragged on, I further defaced the back blank pages of Wendell's book with these thoughts:

> It is a terrible, wrong thing to say and awful to admit, but when I was in the rehabilitation department waiting for the doctor, I watched the other patients and I thought, I cannot bear to turn out like them. One man was in a power wheelchair, tilted back, with a water bottle in the cup holder, a fleece blanket decorated with puppies draped over his legs. A woman was next to him in her wheelchair. She looked un-bathed, with long, grey, unkempt hair and with half a dozen windshield ornaments dangling from the handlebars and what looked like a bunch of garbage stuffed into the basket in the front. I thought, I am not these people. I am reminded of Wendell's word on hierarchy of disability, and I am aware that when it comes to the continuum, I would like to be near one end more than the other. I am educated! I worked at the university; I am completing a graduate degree. I am married, I have a lightweight manual wheelchair, I have been pregnant, I have children, I have three Paralympic medals, I won the President's Service Award, I have even coached non-disabled people. I cannot be that caricature of disability, I cannot embody that stereotype. I am not that. I am not them. I can't be.

> March 21, 2006

> I am horrified with myself. I have realized that the attitude I had about the people I saw in the rehabilitation department the other day is despicable. It is no better than the people who say and believe that they would "rather die than not be able to walk/see/hear." It is not up to me to decide whose bodies are acceptable or unacceptable. I am glad, however, that I learned about this tendency to judge within myself. I am sure I would have denied it if I had ever been accused. I am happy to be aware, so that now I can work on changing this attitude.

I was deeply ashamed of my thoughts that came from a belief that I had more power, status and worth than other people with disabilities. I was embarrassed that I had seen myself as better and more in control than my peers who have disabilities, and yet, I cannot deny how at times during my pregnancy, and later on with my experiences of breastfeeding, the benefits I received from defining myself more as "woman" than "disabled."

Susan Wendell argues that this sort of projection happens all the time but that most of us do not realize it.

> The disciplines of normality, like those of femininity are not only enforced by others but internalized. For many of us, our proximity to the standards of normality is an important aspect of our identity and our sense of social acceptability, an aspect of self-respect...

These reactions are completely understandable, given the disciplines of normality, and they all contribute to the Otherness of people with disabilities.[32]

Writing and reflecting and reading and writing some more about the above thoughts and feelings that I had on being the "Other" made me consider the other ways in which I have experienced this situation before.

She's Starting to Show:
Experiences of Being Seen but Not Heard

Reflecting on the ways I felt once my body was "showing" its pregnancy made me think about the strong memories I have with my body being on display as a young girl. I was just a few weeks shy of completing grade one when my spinal cord was injured. My teacher was a thoughtful woman who rallied my classmates to send homemade cards made from colourful construction paper to the hospital where I was a patient. I remember receiving a card from one of the boys in my class that I ended up keeping for years although I do not have it anymore. On the front of the card he had drawn an empty wheelchair and he had printed underneath the question, "Are You Invisible Now?"

I do not pretend that I have any clues as to why he would ask me such a thing (or why my teacher would allow him to send this to me). I do not know if he thought I now possessed magical powers or whether he actually wondered if my inability to walk somehow made me less important. Whatever the reason, I have often thought about that card and the ways in which having a spinal cord injury renders me both invisible and (ultra) visible at the same time.

When I returned to my elementary school in the fall after the accident, I was sure that my teachers would assert that our school was now accessible to wheelchairs. After all, ramps had been built and a washroom had been renovated in anticipation of my arrival. While the barriers to physical accessibility were easily made, there were many invisible social and attitudinal barriers that created situations of "ultravisibility." General assemblies, for example, brought on some of my greatest discomforts and created some of the biggest inequalities and most noticeable differences between my peers and me. Entering the gym, I would inevitably feel anxious about where to sit. Everyone else would be able to sit on their bums on the gym floor and I would still be sitting in my wheelchair. That act of sitting on the floor would instantly change the height differential — when I was surrounded by standing and walking people, I was the short one; when I was surrounded by people sitting on the floor, I would be the tall one. Instead of feeling tall though, I would just feel awkward, "in the way" and unable to hide. Full of anxiety, I would wish for a way to minimize my wheelchair so that I could somehow blend in. These days, as a mother attending the general assemblies of my school-age son, I can comfortably sit along the sidelines with the teachers and other parents, who usually sit in chairs. Yet, with the experience of childhood anxiety brought on by general assemblies burned into my body's memories, the experience of attending an assembly now, no matter what the subject or theme, inevitably stirs butterflies in my stomach and brings tears to my eyes.

Feminist theory offers some illuminations about invisibility and visibility. While Simone de Beauvoir first suggested that women are not born, but rather made or taught to be female,[33] more recent feminist theorists have taken this point further, suggesting that the female body can also be seen as a "thing" or as an object that is subject to the "male gaze."[34] Furthermore, Marion Young asserts that the notion of the "male gaze" is one of Foucault's disciplinary techniques that strongly influences the way women perceive their body's appearance.[35] The gaze of others is disciplinary and judgmental; when we observe others, we are constantly making assumptions about who and what we think we are seeing. Because I was more acutely aware of my body's femininity and sexuality during pregnancy, I became more sensitive to the way other people perceived my changing body. I realized that I looked like a living contradiction — disabled and pregnant — and that contradiction was pushing others to reconsider and confront their ideas of whom and what I should be. I was also accustomed to concealing my body and minimizing the space that it took up (as I had tried to do during those dreaded general assemblies). Becoming so much obviously bigger and epitomizing the image of femininity (at least in my mind), forced me to confront how visible and how open to the gaze of others I had become.

Living with the Baby Bump

While I was pregnant but before I started to "show," I felt more uncomfortable with my body than I did at any previous point in my life. I was worried that people would just think I was fat, further perpetrating the stereotypical image of a person with a disability as being inactive and physically incompetent, images I had worked hard to change for myself for years, particularly through my involvement with sport.

November 13, 1996

Darrell tries to assure me that I am not getting fat in other areas besides my belly, but I remain very self-conscious. I keep thinking that people will assume I am fat, not pregnant because they will not expect me to be pregnant in the first place. I don't think I am imagining things — I see the looks I get. Some people look surprised, some look confused. I have even seen people do double takes. I wish I could put a sign on my chair that says "You are not imagining things, yes, I am pregnant." Or I could get a t-shirt that says "No longer a virgin." I know that I am awkward at best with this new identity, this role that I also did not expect for myself. I feel that I don't know how to do this pregnancy with grace.

July 3, 2005

For a couple of weeks now, my pants have not fit very well and when I tried to shop at the maternity store, I felt so strange and out of place that I just left without trying anything on or buying anything. In fact, now that I think about it, I felt like an imposter!

This weekend though, after seeing me enlarge my pants with elastic bands in order to make them fit around my expanding belly, Darrell insisted that we shop at the maternity store together. He blazed a trail right into the store and kept taking things off the racks and piling them into a dressing room. He came into the dressing room with me and helped me try on a bunch of different things. He was quick with his appraisals — he either liked or disliked and then made piles depending on his assessment. He looked like he was having a great time. He even put the pregnancy pillow around his own stomach to see what he would look like if he had a belly like mine. He looked hilarious! With all of our laughing and carrying on, we made a lot of noise. I think the staff that work there were surprised he came into the change room with me in the first place. In the end, we bought 3 pair of pants and 2 blouses. I even wore the new jeans out of the store.

The experience made me feel more legitimately pregnant somehow, like it validated that very female experience.

During pregnancy, particularly the latter months when a woman starts to show, women are confronted with constant and intense physical transformations, emotional upheavals and social changes. Amy Mullin argues that the study of both able-bodied and disabled women's experiences with pregnancy is both rare and new and not enough is known about how it affects a woman's sense of herself as a female.[36] Mullin also states that because pregnancy is such a meaningful embodied experience, it is important to look at all kinds of contexts (e.g., social, cultural) because there will not be "such a thing as a typical experience of pregnancy."[37]

One social change that some feminist theorists argue is that a tension exists for pregnant women between being seen as a mother and being seen as sexual and desirable because there is a sharp distinction between the two images.[38] This might explain the shift in recent years in media images from pregnant women wearing over-sized, flowing garments to tight, skin- and belly-baring clothes. I suspect that at least one of the reasons for this tension is that non-disabled women are assumed to be sexual prior to being pregnant and we do not usually expect mothers to be sexual. However, this does not speak to my experience. Because I was not previously seen as a sexual person, my pregnancy, especially once I started to show, revealed something about me that was not expected: that I *was* actually a sexual person. In short, where some pregnant non-disabled women experience a loss of sexual and feminine identity, I experienced a gain.

When You Are Not Expected to Be Expecting: Fear of Public Reaction

At the same time that my sexuality and femininity were being confirmed in many ways, I was also deeply concerned that others might negatively perceive my pregnancy. I was anxious that strangers would just think I was fat, a fear that is based in a societal view of people with disabilities, especially women, as passive, weak and inactive.[39] My anxiety was sometimes confirmed by how others interacted with me. I was anxious that I was going to be judged; that people were thinking I should not be allowed to mother and that I did not deserve that role.

> January 2, 1997
>
> I need a new bra. My rib cage is expanding to make room for Pat. So I went to the maternity store. Isn't that what pregnant women do? There were three salespeople and no one would help me, so I approached one of them, saying I did not know what size I should buy. She said, with surprise, "Oh! Are you expecting?" I was stunned. I am in a fucking maternity store. I am seven months pregnant. Look at me! How did she think I was going to respond? "Oh, sorry, I thought I was in Zellers?" She just thought I was fat, I guess. A different woman ended up helping me and I did buy a bra in the end.

I was also worried that others would perceive my pregnancy as something I did not deserve and that I was causing an unnecessary burden on society, due to medical and healthcare intervention. In short, I feared a public perception that I would not be able to take care of my child independently. Many argue that women who become mothers are subject to surveillance by the public, because we monitor their size, weight, the food they eat, the activities they do and the clothes they wear. We judge them on whether or not they want a home or hospital delivery, whether or not they use a doctor, midwife or doula, and if they choose to breast or bottle-feed. Disability theorist, Carol Thomas, argues that pregnant women with disabilities are particularly vulnerable to scrutiny.[40]

I was also concerned with how others would react to the news that I was pregnant. Whereas most women who have planned pregnancies expect to experience a positive response from others, I was on guard for the potential negative response each time I told someone. I was fortunate that the nurse who did the pregnancy test for me was also a good friend. While her news affirming my pregnancy was shocking to me, having her emotion-filled and sincerely positive response to the news definitely made the moment easier and even memorable. Similarly, telling my family, co-workers and friends was a positive experience. They were congratulatory and, although many of them were surprised by our news, they seemed genuinely pleased for both Darrell and me.

> June 22, 2005
>
> When I went to J's thesis defence this afternoon, Kent stopped me and commented on my need to delay my proposal. I told him that I am pregnant. His response was so positive; his smile spoke volumes. I was so worried about what his reaction was going to be. His reaction was simple in a way, after all, people smile all the time when they hear a woman is pregnant. But because I have a lot of respect for his opinions, because I am in the middle of my graduate studies, a SSHRC scholar, and yes, yes, yes, because I am a paraplegic, his reaction to this news really mattered to me. I do not think I will ever be able to fully thank him for doing the right thing at the right time.

However, not all responses were happy ones. "Oh dear" were the first words out of the mouth of the doctor I saw after I learned I was pregnant the first time. Similarly, "You have certainly complicated your life" were the first words my doctor said when he learned of my second pregnancy.

> May 29, 2005
>
> I am officially 10 weeks pregnant; the baby is an inch long and about the size of a walnut. More people know and I am okay with that. I need to tell the kids I help coach and I need to tell my own team and Finn, of course. I told my other coach over the phone. He was civil, but he didn't even wish us congratulations. Instead, he just commented a few times about how shooting is no longer a priority for me.
>
> Honestly, for all the warm and enthusiastic responses we have had, there have also been many cool, negative and judgmental comments. Other people have frowned, or given me a look that I can't quite explain, but it certainly isn't a happy look.

On one hand, my disability and my wheelchair represent my constant visibility especially as I encounter barriers in space and architecture. Paradoxically, the ways in which I am ignored, silenced, disrespected and not understood as a disabled person, and as a disabled woman, are symbols of my invisibility. "Women's bodies may be highly noticed, yet their capacities, lives and desires unseen."[41]

Spare the Child/Spoil the Rods

As I said in the beginning of this chapter, this was probably the hardest section to write and reflect on. My journals are often written in during the "heat of the moment" and in the middle of crisis. I faced a particular crisis during my second pregnancy.

Early on I sensed that something was not "right" with my body. I was suddenly experiencing autonomic dysreflexia on a regular basis; an indication that there was something wrong below the level of my injury that I could not detect, but was being alerted to nonetheless.

May 25, 2005

I have hit the wall. Last night I could not find a restful or comfortable position. Impossible! My body cannot be still. It spasms and jerks constantly. The lack of sleep caught up with me and I cried for hours. I feel so betrayed and alone when this happens. I feel like I have nowhere to turn and it is terrifying. I finally fell asleep around 4 a.m. and I was shaken awake with spasms again shortly after 7. Something doesn't feel quite right about this. Once I took Patrick to school, I came home to try to sleep awhile, but the same thing happened, not surprising, but since I was already upset, I continued crying. It has been months since I have had a good night's sleep.

August 6, 2005

Tonight Pat and I are at Mom and Dad's on the farm. I have had a hard time when I have to be somewhere that is not particularly accessible. The bathroom here is big enough but the transfers are different than at home and that makes everything awkward right now. Plus, just when I thought my rib pain was as bad as it could get, it got worse. I am having sharp, stabbing pains in my chest. I need to go to physiotherapy next week and I will go home to Saskatoon early if I need to.

August 7, 2005

I had another tough day. This time it is my bladder. I am having a lot of profuse sweats and I feel what is a bit like a slight bladder spasm off and on all day. I don't know if it is a spasm or some other kind of discomfort.

October 2, 2005

This is my second night in the hospital. My body is completely unpredictable, bizarre and incredibly difficult to figure out. I have an on-going high fever, my back is having a lot of pain, especially on the right side, my heart rate is very high, ranging between 110-140 bpm, I am short of breath, and my posture has become very crooked. We are exploring infection and blood clots. Further, since the indwelling catheter came out on Wednesday, I have not had one single bladder spasm, not one single sweat. My feet are even dry. I have been incontinent twice, I didn't feel a thing. I also had a pelvic exam and I didn't feel a thing. Nothing. My sensation is completely gone.

I hated those spasms and those sweats. Now that they're gone, I am scared. I am scared that I have lost the sensation forever. One resident doctor thinks it is all a coincidence. This is shocking to me. I absolutely do not think it is a coincidence and that the AD is connected to my bladder, something I have maintained all along. Why doesn't anybody listen to me? I know my body better than anyone. Why don't they even ask for my opinion? I am starting to feel really scared.

October 12, 2005

I have been back in the hospital for a few days now.

We were waiting on this final test to let us know if the pain and the fevers were due to an infection in my back from the fracture of my rods, or from injuries I sustained here from this inaccessible room last week. One of Dr. O's residents was here to tell me. Then she asked whether I had four rods or two. I felt an overwhelming sense of dread and I answered, "two." She looked a bit confused, then said as if it were the simplest thing in the world, "I distinctly saw four," then showed me in the air with her fingers where they were placed. That little air drawing upset me beyond words. This is how I learned that the rods had moved apart. I can't believe she told me in this way. Doesn't she have an idea of how horrible this is?

I don't know what it all means, but I know it isn't good. No, this is very, very bad news for me. I don't know what it means for the baby. I need a good cry and I can't do that with Darrell because Patrick is always here when Darrell is here. Pat sees me in enough pain, this is not a "normal" home life situation, I have enough vulnerability with him around. I can't break down sobbing too.

However, he is sensitive to my emotions (he wanted to know why I am sad even though I wasn't crying) and I felt that he needed to know the truth. Tonight I told him about my broken rods. I told him as honestly and simply as I could. I said, "Honey, the rods in my back have broken. We do not know why. It may have happened even if I was not pregnant. We cannot do surgery to fix the rods while the baby is still inside me, but once she is born, I will need a big operation."

He just held his head in his hands. He said he wasn't sad about being afraid of how I may not be able to look after him, nor was he sad about being afraid that I wouldn't be there for him. Instead, he said in a sure, strong, and steady voice that he knew I was always with him and will always be there for him. He is sad, he told me, because he is afraid of all the pain I will have. Then he crawled into bed with me and I held him in my arms. We stayed like that for a long time and I stroked his hair and kissed his cheek.

I intended to sing him a song to make him feel better, but what actually happened was one of those precious mother-child bonding moments that I am sure I will always remember. I sang/prayed to my boy-child, my un-born child and me:

Ooh, child, things are gonna get easier
Ooh child, things will get lighter
Someday we'll walk in the rays of the beautiful sun
(The Five Stairsteps, "Ooh Child")

I cannot read the above journal passages without tears brimming in my eyes. Those are raw words that sear the paper in my journal, and they appear on the pages without the consolation of time to soften or heal them. I have frequently written in my journals right in the moment, not later in the day when I have had time to think, reflect or contain my emotion. In re-reading these and other stories about my pregnancy with Chelsea, for example, I see how relatively quickly my back's steel hardware broke, how quickly my spine became unstable, and how it felt like I became morbidly crooked overnight and it terrifies me, even now, almost three years later, that it might happen again. Every sharp pain, every excessive sweat and every creak and groan my bones make threaten to shatter my inner sovereignty. Survival takes strength, faith and the ability to be comfortable with the uncomfortable, which are many of the qualities I learned as an athlete. Survival means I am in control, if not of the situation and the things that happen to me, then at least of how I manage those situations, how I see them and live with them. Audre Lorde said that "I am not only a casualty, I am also a warrior."[42]

In many ways, I certainly was a casualty. At the beginning of this chapter I recalled my challenging medical experiences and outlined how women with disabilities are subjugated to what Michel Foucault calls the "discipline" of medical systems. This discipline exerts significant social pressure to "shape, regulate, and normalize subjugated bodies."[43] I definitely feel that this was a large part of my pregnancy experience. However, at the same time, I believe I was also a warrior because just as significant to my experience was my drive for personal choice and free will. It has been argued that one of the limitations of a Foucaudian perspective is its disregard for human agency and individual resistance to the disciplines and their power.[44] After all, there are numerous (and many famous) testimonies that detail how human beings are complex, multi-faceted people who can be controlled, regulated and oppressed while at the same time as we can be strong, resistant and in control of our choices. Despite its apparent or assumed docility, it is equally important to note that mine was also an active body capable of exercising free will and making conscious choices about my situations. My practical embodied experience of disability and pregnancy, however, was often lived in the juxtaposition of these two theoretical positions — individual autonomy versus the overarching predisposition against disability. Many of the above personal stories are about things that were done to me, how I was victimized and oppressed, and yet, there is also much evidence to my individual agency, like how I dealt with my ultrasound technician's biases and the way in which I told my son about my broken steel hardware. So although it makes me sad to read about it, and it makes me angry to write about how I was sometimes treated, I am also comforted to see in my journals my many acts of what I consider to be strength, and how I knew that I should not be dismissed and underestimated.

You've been wrong too long
I'm full of emotion
and stuff you can't contain
But you can't make me go away
(Bad Religion, "Don't Sell Me Short")

4

It's Time!

My Birthing Stories

While I worked at the University of Saskatchewan, I once had the opportunity to hire several people at one time, and during that search I conducted over forty-five interviews. One of the more unconventional questions I always asked was: "What is the bravest thing you have ever done?" During one of my de-briefing meetings about the candidates, one of my colleagues on the hiring committee who was intrigued by my odd questions, turned to me and asked, "Heather, I am curious — what is the bravest thing *you* have ever done?" Without having consciously thought about my own answer prior to this, I nonetheless responded without hesitation, "Two things. Getting involved in wheelchair sports and making the decision to have a baby." These two ideas that seem to have nothing in common with one another are linked in my mind because both becoming involved with sport and making the decision to have a baby required me to extend the ideas of what I expected for my life and beyond what others expected of me. "Female, disabled, and dark bodies are supposed to be dependent, incomplete, vulnerable, and incompetent bodies."[1] Both sport and my decision to become a mother required me to re-define who I thought I was. After having read, reflected and written about my childbirth experiences, I also see how often I both unconsciously and consciously used sport terminology and "shooting talk" throughout. It is with these reflections in mind that I constructed this chapter.

The One-Shot Match

The one-shot match is a concept that Finn introduced to me early on in my shooting career. It is simply the precise process a shooter determines is the necessary one to achieve a successful shot. Understanding the components that achieve a perfect shot in a one-shot match is really about breaking down an experience into a series of moments. The theory is that if you can establish the steps that are necessary to accomplish a perfect shot, then that process can be dissected, piece by piece, and a strategy can be developed. This does not mean a perfect shot happens in the same way for everyone — on the contrary, every shooter will have a different way of seeing and a different way of positioning herself. Nor does it mean that once the perfect way has been established, it will never change. To be successful, one has to be open to revisions and change when the timing is right. However, in critical moments, the one-shot match should be the process one has come to believe is effective and reliable.

This all sounds very technical, and in most ways it is. However, the one-shot match is also a mental process and is really about focusing on the present moment. Refining it became a large part of my mental training exercises, but the practice also extended over into my everyday life. I cannot count the number of times I would go to my one-shot match in my head when I needed something to focus on, or because the steps always have a concentration on breath-watching, when I simply needed to relax enough to fall asleep. The magic of the one-shot match and living in the moment for me was that I was also able to take the skills of living a one-shot match and apply them to having ownership over my birthing experiences.

Going with the Flow

The sport psychology training I received as an athlete provided me with invaluable skills to deal with the physical difficulties I encountered while I was pregnant. How I learned to lower my heart rate and relax for shooting was key to managing the difficulties my body was having during pregnancy and in childbirth. The skills of being able to re-frame and re-focus during a competition were also useful during pregnancy and childbirth. I was able to mentally deconstruct moments of crisis, which was critical to my ability to cope with pain and emotionally trying times. Self-talk in particular was an important tool that I used while I was an athlete. Simon Jenkins describes self-talk as a tool that athletes can use to focus attention, provide motivation and strengthen self-confidence.[2]

When Finn first introduced me to the concept of self-talk, I was immediately intrigued. Self-talk came naturally to me since I had been using music as a form of self-talk for years. My dad had encouraged me to "plant a song" in my head while I was training and competing, so incorporating words was a relatively easy transition. Canadian sport psychologist Terry Orlick describes self-talk as a tactic that encourages confidence in an athlete by concentrating on positive beliefs the athlete has about his or her abilities.[3] Those beliefs should be grounded, Orlick says, on real past histories of successful outcomes. Furthermore, many athletes use the practice of self-talk to enter into "flow," what Jenkins considers to be an "altered state of consciousness" or "total unity, inner strength and wholeness of being, as well as a loss of fears, inhibitions, and insecurities."[4] My ability to use self-talk to enter the "flow" experience was a significant contribution to what I consider to be the best competitive performance of my shooting career.

September 13, 1992

I made the final again — this time in the co-ed 3 position! I was so surprised and I did not expect that I would make the final so I even had my gear already packed up and was ready to sit in the stands and watch all the excitement, not be part of the excitement! But Finn came running towards me with my equipment bag and told me to get suited up — I don't know who was more caught off guard, him or me. I was known as a pistol shooter, not really a rifle shooter, so a lot of people who came to watch the final did not even know or realize who I was.

I was last in the final, eighth, and the only girl, and the only North American. All the other finalists were men from Europe. My sighting shots were absolutely awful, all over the place, and I knew that if I wanted any self respect at the end of all of this, I had better get my shit together. So I tried to settle down, relax, and remember my one-shot match. My one-shot match allowed me to see my shot, feel my shot, and even hear my shot. Several deep breaths later, my first shot on target was gone… and it was a good one (10.5). In fact, it was the best one of all 8 of us.

About shot #4, the crowd turned my way, cheering the loudest for the lone Canadian girl on the end, shooting her heart out. And my heart was out — it was beating so hard, there was no time or point in getting it to quiet down, I just went with it instead. As a result, I would raise my rifle into position, get on target, feel that crazy heartbeat, and have to lower the gun again. I took all my 75 seconds that are allowed, and expended twice the energy that should have been needed. My face was so hot and flushed that the cheek piece would slip around my face and I had to wipe it down with my glove. I was sweating so hard that some of the perspiration would slip around the head band that held my eye patch and drip into my eye, stinging me. Despite all this though, my shots were strong, I could call all of them, and they were all solid 10's. Between shots, I would close my eyes and see, feel and hear the 10's. Using self-talk, I just kept repeating "I am calm, cool and confident" and for some reason it was important to me to not just say it in my head but to mumble it to myself. I swear I could also feel Finn having a heart attack behind me in the stands. My shots were fantastic, and the crowd was roaring every time I took one, chanting "Can-a-da"!

In the end, I moved up two spots to place 6th, but the best part was my high final score. I am so impressed with myself for getting focused and staying calm and confident. Why do personal bests have to require so much work? I really did not know I had it in me, to tell the truth. I had no idea my body could make such an amazing thing happen. I had to do it to believe it.

Finn is just beside himself with pride. He was holding the video camera but the footage shows a lot of shaking and jumping up and down by the cameraman.

According to Jerry Lynch and Chungliang Huang, the words we say to ourselves can be used as a powerful tool to enhance performance, and often act as an energizer, problem solver and controller of physiological responses.[5] Through the words and images I chose to use, I was able to both take responsibility and credit for the successful outcome. What I could not have anticipated was how critical self-talk and entering into flow would be to me when I gave birth to Patrick.

Patrick's Birth

March 29, 1997

It is 9:05 p.m. and I am breastfeeding my son. He is about 17 hours old.

At midnight Darrell and I decided to go to the hospital as I was having what I thought were violent bladder spasms. Not knowing what labour pains would feel like, I thought I was having another bladder infection. We called Dr. T first as I was reluctant to go to the hospital in the middle of the night for what I thought would result in a course of antibiotics. We arrived around 1:00 a.m. and Dr. T announced to us that I was having "8 cm dilated bladder spasms." I went into the delivery room and Dr. T asked me if I wanted to try and push. I told him I did not know how because everyone thought my body was incapable of that. We had not attended pre-natal classes because we were told that the pushing would not apply to me so there would be no point in learning about it. Nevertheless, Dr. T told me to try. Why not?

After a brief tutorial, a contraction came but my first attempt at pushing did not work. Dr. T, knowing my sports background, said, "Okay, we are going to try this again but with a little visualization. We are going to put your sport mental training into practice." He painted me a picture of what needed to happen and we waited for the next contraction. This time I was ready. Darrell held my legs and braced my back. I held on to the sides of the bed and pushed. I had the one-shot match that Dr. T helped me build and that became my focus. It was hard work. Using all the strength I had in my arms, shoulders, hands, even my face and neck, I bared down and pushed until sweat plastered my hair against my head. In between contractions I was in Barcelona on the shooting line, relaxed, focused and set on my task. I kept saying out loud, "Yes," "I can do this," "I am strong," and "My body can do this." I was so pleased and surprised that I could progress the birth by pushing.

Darrell and I were amazed. We actively pushed this way for about 45 minutes, and then Dr. T told me to reach down with my hand and touch Pat's head. He said he had never seen a mom's reaction quite like mine before — total shock. It is true; I was still dumbfounded that my body was actually making this event happen! At the very end, Dr. T thought he should assist the baby with a little bit of vacuuming. And the next thing we knew, our baby boy was born. Dr. T clamped the umbilical cord and Darrell did the cutting. We called our parents to give them the news. My mom cried with relief.

Because we decided at the last minute to not have an epidural, my blood pressure was monitored throughout the delivery to be sure it would not go too high due to the pain. It went high, but not so much that any intervention was needed. Everyone had believed that I would need an epidural to control for pain, an IV and a foley catheter. I did not need any of these things. All I really needed was a doctor who believed in the abilities of my body, a pair of strong arms, a lot of husband support and a good mental plan.

I had exerted so much physical energy that my blood pressure dropped drastically low, so low it did not even register at first. Yet, I felt fantastic, like I had just had completed the final of the most intense match of my life. What a miracle. My body did not fail me. My body worked. My body worked well. I pushed! Me!

Until I started the process of selecting journal entries into themes for my thesis, I had not fully considered the parallels between these above two experiences. This process involves "rewriting of the self and the social,"[6] and an ability to go beyond the everyday stories of one's life, especially those stories that have been told many times, and deeply reflect on the reasons why those stories hold meaning. Both of the above stories I had told many times. Both of these stories illustrate moments of high drama where I pushed my body's abilities to its limits. Both gave me the opportunity to test my mental toughness. Both experiences culminated in great "wins." This, I think, is obvious.

What is probably less conspicuous, however, is the magic that happens in telling the stories *to* someone. My listener is almost always captivated, entertained and surprised. I love this inevitable reaction of the listener because both the stories and the reaction to them reinforce who I sketch myself to be — strong, unexpected and interesting; characteristics that are usually the opposite of who we expect people with disabilities to be.[7] Arthur Frank would also argue that, through such stories, bonds of empathy are created through the teller and the listener and "the circle of shared experience widens."[8] This is a way, he says, that my body, which is oftentimes silenced, can speak and be heard. I believe that the telling of these stories allows my body to be seen, or perceived, in different, more positive and definitely unexpected ways. It is these unexpected ways of strength and remarkable physical ability that I want to be seen as having after so many years of having received the message that mine was a body not made for such extraordinary experiences. "People do not make up their stories by themselves. The shape of telling is molded by all the rhetorical expectations that the storyteller has been internalizing ever since he heard some relative describe an illness, or she saw her first television commercial for a non-prescription remedy."[9]

Oh, Come On, There Is More to It than That

What is also less obvious (at least initially to me) is the other factor that contributed to the successful or happy ending to these stories. When I deeply think and reflect, I am honest both to myself and to the words I write down. When I first did this, it suddenly occurred to me that it was more than self-talk that culminated in those successful outcomes. I then thought the other factor must have been pure grit, toughness or an ability to "dig deep" or "suck it up" and get it done. While I think it is true that I have that ability to draw on inner resources in critical times, as many of us do, the truth is that when I contemplated that idea for a while another honest factor was revealed to me. And that was simply my zealous desire and deep-seated drive to "win." When I was in the final with all those older, seasoned European men and when I was pushing my body to independently deliver Patrick into this world, I wanted to win. I wanted to succeed, to accomplish something extraordinary that would allow me a great story that I would never tire of telling.

Chelsea's Birth

With the high drama test of mental toughness and physical exertion that Patrick's delivery necessitated in mind, I prepared for Chelsea's birth. Although I knew my body was now different and therefore the delivery would also be different, my other experience with childbirth was the only information I had to draw on to help me prepare. I once again drew on my history with sport to work on this preparation.

> November 27, 2005
>
> To tell the truth, I feel like I am preparing for a competition tomorrow. My mind frame is changing. I am getting mentally tough, strong, and ready. I have rehearsed my one-shot match. I am anticipatory, but I am also relaxed — my ideal performance state. Focused. Clear. Ready. A gold medal performance, a personal best, awaits. That's my mind, my mental preparation. As for my body? No problem: it has been training for months.

Using terminology and processes that I would employ for competition felt comfortable during my second pregnancy and childbirth experience. Simply, if it had worked before, I thought it could work again. I again turned to my one-shot match for giving birth: what steps did I have control over, how could I best maximize my body and mind towards a successful birth? The lessons I learned in sport are with me all the time and it is a powerful feeling to be able to draw on them for dealing with life events that seem to have nothing to do with sport.

These lessons were intensely tested during the last trimester of my pregnancy with Chelsea. The broken steel hardware in my back was causing autonomic dysreflexia every day, all day long. There was no relief. I was dealing with excessive sweats that would leave my pillow case soaked after only a few hours of sleep. I would have to change it in the middle of the night; oftentimes I also slept with a towel on top of the pillow case. I had to change my shirt several times a day because it would be so wet that you could actually ring out perspiration like a wet towel. As a result, I was often shivering from cold. Accompanying this was a fever that for some reason would start every day in the late afternoon. I had a high resting heart rate all day and night long (around 140 beats per minute). Due to the broken hardware that had damaged my spinal cord, I had lost all my bladder sensation. It was especially because of this fact that I was convinced I would not be able to detect when I was in labour. After all, the sensations of what I thought were strong bladder spasms was how I felt at the beginning of labour with Patrick. I was sure that because I did not have this physical feeling anymore, that I would not be able to "tell" when labour was starting with this baby. Over and over again I was assured by the nursing staff and my doctor, as well as family and friends, that I would most definitely know when labour was happening. "You know your body so well," they would tell me, "so try not to worry." "You will feel the contractions. Your belly will get hard as a rock, and you will know." I remained unconvinced. Unbeknownst to me so did my husband.

I got up in the morning one day to find the *What to Expect When You Are Expecting* book open to the chapter on emergencies and what would happen if a woman has no choice but to have her baby at home. Darrell confessed that he had been reading the book in the middle of the night because he was too worried to sleep. This was a sign to me that I needed to try to convince my obstetrician that my labour should be induced. However, my obstetrician completely disagreed, telling me that induction was not the best route for the baby and if this was a spinal cord-related issue, I had to take it up with my rehabilitation doctor. Having my thoughts completely dismissed by my doctor is one example of how patients are expected to be compliant to their doctor's orders.

Talcott Parsons was arguably the first social scientist to theorize this kind of doctor-patient relationship and his ideas have had a profound impact on medical theory and practice for decades. According to him, a central part of being sick is submitting to the care of a doctor.[10] Arthur Frank argues that the "postmodern experience of illness begins when ill people recognize that more is involved in their experiences than the medical story can tell."[11] Arthur Frank also argues that physicians as described by Parson's sociology are more accountable to professional policies than to individual patients.[12] This is certainly how I felt when I left my obstetrician's office and I wondered if he had heard a word I had said. However, I did quickly take the matter up with Dr. L, my rehabilitation doctor. I remember feeling relieved and respected as he listened without interruption about my fears of not being able to detect labour. He said he would write my obstetrician a letter stating that it was his belief that I should be induced at thirty-seven weeks so that the conditions were under control. My appointment with Dr. L was on a Friday afternoon. To my pleasant surprise, he asked me if it would be okay if my obstetrician would get the letter on Monday. I smiled, with deep relief, and said that I thought that would be just fine.

So at thirty-seven weeks, I was scheduled for induction. My obstetrician was out of the city so I was assigned someone new with whom I felt quite comfortable even though I had only met her once before. In the morning, I received oxytocin, a drug typically used for induction, and although my water broke fairly early, no contractions accompanied it. In my room was Darrell, Patrick and Jody, a close family friend who Patrick chose to accompany him should he need any support (assuming that his dad would be busy with me). By dinner time that evening, no contractions were happening, so my new obstetrician said we would try a more aggressive route the next day. Thinking the baby was not on her way, the doctor left to go home.

Soon after, a nurse came in to check on the baby's heart rate with an ultrasound. When she was unable to find the heart rate, Darrell started to look worried. Sensing that something was up, Jody wisely took Patrick for a walk down the hall. I was feeling suddenly nauseated and I wondered if it had anything to do with my position in the bed. Keeping the bed sheet draped over myself, I turned from side to side, all the while feeling that I might vomit. Darrell asked the nurse to call the resident doctor and she quickly obliged. We both got the sense that she was also nervous about not being able to find the baby's heart rate. When the resident came in to see me, she took charge and used the ultrasound wand herself. There was still no detection of a heart rate. With Darrell right next to me on one side, and the nurse on the other, the resident doctor asserted that she was going to do an exam of my cervix. When she swiftly drew back my bed sheet, she shouted, "The baby's head is out. This baby needs to be delivered now. Call NICU [neo-natal intensive care unit] stat!"

I watched Darrell's face drain of blood; he became as white as the sheet that had just been removed from my lower body. Strangely, my own face seemed to contain all its blood plus his — all of a sudden I felt very red and flushed. Tears sprung to my eyes, but I would not allow myself to cry. "There is no time for tears," I told myself. On my doctor's orders, I pushed like I had learned to do on the delivery table some nine years before, relying on the visualization techniques that I had firmly burned into my subconscious mind, and my baby slid out. Darrell recovered, and sped out of the room to shout for Jody and Patrick who came at once. Our baby was checked over with the assertive speed reserved for emergencies and was declared miraculously and absolutely perfect.

Almost immediately I expressed my gratitude towards Dr. L for listening to me and believing me when I told him I would not detect labour. Without the controlled conditions of the induction, I most assuredly would have given birth to this baby at home, on the toilet, or in the middle of the night. The consequences could have been disastrous. Darrell and I remain grateful to him to this very day.

November 28, 2005

All in all, a 10.9 delivery, just a bit different from my one-shot match... Welcome, little girl.

These are days you'll remember
Never before and never since, I promise
will the whole world be warm as this
(Natalie Merchant, "These Are Days")

5

Inaccessibility

Shut up!
You're talking too loud
Get back in your corner
(The Au Pairs, "Stepping Out of Line")

I deal with inaccessibility issues on a daily basis. Because they are so prevalent, many times I am not bothered by them in a significant way. However, sometimes I get angry and frustrated. Other times I end up feeling quite hurt and small. I have a long list of inaccessibility frustrations and offer a selection from it:

I am told that I should have a physical examination once a year, but I cannot get on to my doctor's examination table because it is too high. I asked him what it would take to acquire a bed that raises and lowers in his clinic, and he scoffed at the idea, telling me that a $5000 bed was just too expensive to justify.

I have never found a gravel or sand-free playground where I can push my kids on the swings.

I cannot guarantee that I will be able to park in the designated spot for wheelchairs at my son's school despite the fact that I am the only parent there who uses a wheelchair. There are no children who use wheelchairs in the school either. Non-disabled parents are always vying for the spot. A few months ago I was given the finger by one mom when I told her (gently, mind you) that she did not have the legal right to park there.

There are stairs getting into nearly every dance studio and gymnastic club in the city. What will I do when Chelsea wants to do these activities?

Last weekend's paper's headline indicated that the major multi-million dollar development taking place in our city's downtown will only have stairs because a ramp would take away from the aesthetics of the design.

During my pregnancies and childbirths, inaccessibility was even more of an issue because my body had changed. My ability to feel balanced was altered because I had a new centre of gravity with my baby belly. I experienced so many difficulties with inaccessible spaces and inaccessible attitudes during this time, and wrote about it often in my journals.

Inaccessibility issues began before I even went home from the hospital. When I was first injured, there were many physical and attitudinal barriers to integrating me back into the community and, as a consequence, my parents quickly found themselves in the roles of advocates. For example, after watching me "attend" my science and art classes alone in a tiny dark room by way of a closed circuit television, while the rest of my classmates participated in the upstairs classroom, my parents pushed our public school board to install a wheelchair lift in my junior high school. When they believed it was no longer acceptable to have my brother, Jim, or my cousins carry me on and off the school bus, they insisted on having a bus with an integrated wheelchair lift transport me to and from school. Both times my parents were met with great resistance from the powers that held the money that was needed to make these changes. Eventually they were successful and, since then, many people have used the accessibility.

Sometimes the advocacy was even messier than just dealing with the bureaucracy of a school board. My dad once passionately expressed his contempt for a man who had illegally parked in a wheelchair parking stall and the ensuing altercation came to blows. My mom continually spoke up for me with doctors, physiotherapists and occupational therapists. My parents became advocates whether they were comfortable with the roles or not, and whether they intended to or not. Because of their advocacy, many parts of our community changed for the better. They deserve credit for making tremendous alterations to the accessibility in both in my life and in our community.

> *I've got a good father*
> *and his strength is what makes me cry*
> *I've got a good mother*
> *and her voice is what keeps me here*
> *(Jann Arden, "Good Mother")*

Inaccessibility of Public Spaces

As an adult, the role of advocate rests primarily with me. Access is so central to my daily life that I have learned to expect inaccessibility rather than the opposite in public places such as restaurants, stores and even hospitals. While access issues are pervasive and emerge in a variety of everyday situations, my pregnancies brought forward a new set of accessibility issues. Public places, especially doctors' offices and hospitals, the spaces that are supposed to cater to the health and safety of all persons, were particularly frustrating.

September 27, 1996

> My new doctor's office does not have an accessible bed — one that is low enough to get on and off of. Normally I would have been able to do the transfer, but once I have the extra belly weight it will be too difficult, I'm sure. He says this is no problem because there is a regular bed — the type you might have in a bedroom — just down the hall and although it might be a bit awkward for him to examine me there, he will gladly do it.

My pregnant belly changed my physicality in ways that altered my sense of balance and my centre of gravity. I could not perform the kind of athletic/risky transfers I was used to doing before I was pregnant. If I fell I would not only endanger my well-being but also that of my unborn child. My doctors' offices did not have accessible examination tables; this was also true for some of the ultrasound tables I needed to use. While the delivery tables would raise and lower to a safe and correct height, the beds in the ante-partum and post-partum hospital units did not. Furthermore, most of the bathrooms located in the delivery rooms and hospital rooms contained grab bars in incorrect places and toilets that were low and, therefore, dangerous to use, particularly when one has a large pregnant belly to negotiate or when one has just given birth and is weak and sore.

January 2, 1997

> We also did a tour of the birthing rooms. The bathrooms appear accessible, even some with wheel-in showers. The nurses we spoke to felt we should skip assessment and go straight to delivery since assessment is not accessible at all. We learned a lot.

Wendell argues that while feminists contend that the world has been planned and created for the male body, disability theorists feel that the social world has been and often continues to be constructed "as though everyone were physically strong, as though all bodies were shaped the same, as though everyone could walk, hear, and see well, as though everyone could work and play at a pace that is not compatible with any kind of illness or pain, as though no one were ever dizzy or incontinent or simply needed to lie down."[1] It is often incorrectly assumed that if there is a grab bar in a bathroom, even if that grab bar is ill placed or unsafely attached to the wall, then that bathroom is accessible. This situation is not just limited to spaces and architecture. "The entire physical and social organization of life tends to assume that we are either strong and healthy and able to do what the average young, non-disabled man can do or that we are completely unable to participate in public life."[2]

March 30, 1997

I have just given birth but my baby Patrick and we are going home. My hospital room is just not accessible to me. The bed is not the right height, the bathroom does not have grab bars in the right place, and the toilet is too low. I learned that after the baby is born, a woman's ligaments are stretched; plus she is tired, physically drained. I needed things to be as accessible as possible to avoid injury. I really could have used more time in hospital, but because I need access, we decided to go home where I know I can transfer safely.

Some of the most difficult parts of my second pregnancy were seeing that in terms of the accessibility of the maternity ward at our hospital, nothing had changed in the eight years since I had my first baby. This seemed impossible to believe. Surely I was not the only paraplegic who had been pregnant and had given birth during this time. Did not anyone else experience these problems with the too small bathroom, the low toilets, the incorrectly positioned grab bars and the beds that did not lower enough?

Inaccessible Attitudes

Eight years later, and despite a push towards "universal design" (and perhaps predictably), the accessibility of the hospital had not changed to accommodate pregnant women with disabilities. Similarly, positive attitudes towards disabled mothers-to-be were not universally embraced. While I was fortunate to have an obstetrician during my first pregnancy who was open to having a patient with a spinal cord injury and who was willing to learn what he needed to in order to provide care to me and my unborn baby, I was not so lucky during my second pregnancy. My new doctor was unwilling to discuss my spinal cord-related issues as they affected my pregnancy. He quickly separated his responsibility to the reproductive parts of my body from the non-productive parts of my body. Although he claimed that this was because my rehabilitation doctor was the expert in spinal cord-related issues whereas he was not, I could not help but wonder if it was more a reluctance to acknowledge my disability. Gill writes that some doctors are honest about their discomfort when working with women who have disabilities and their complaints, especially when those health issues include reproduction.[3] Gill also asserts that some health professionals appear to be uneasy with the idea that reproductive health or sexuality could possibly be important to their patients with disabilities.

May 4, 2005

Darrell and I saw our obstetrician specialist today. He questioned us as to why Dr. V had made the referral. I was honest and told him that we questioned her on the decision too. His response was that I was "too complicated, too special" and that he wasn't "smart enough" to handle my pregnancy. It hurt that he didn't even want to discuss the matter with us, but like I told our new doctor, I respect his decision if he is not confident. I talked to him about the dysreflexia I keep having and he quickly dismissed the idea that he could help me figure any of that out at all. This is a job for my rehab doctor, he says. I don't think he is necessarily wrong, I just didn't like his tone or how he made me feel, like I was asking for more than I deserved and like I should not be taking up his time with spinal cord-related questions. He also did not know, or have any ideas about where we would do any of my physical examinations since there were no beds that raised or lowered. I feel like he didn't even try to help us come up with a solution. I could probably get up on the table now; however, I won't once the baby starts to grow.

My doctor's discomfort likely comes from a prevailing social expectation that assumes that pregnant women and infant and children's caregivers should and will be women without disabilities.[4] "When disability and impairment are discussed, they are typically presented as features of fetuses that should be avoided or that justify abortion, rather than as characteristics of children [or] caregivers."[5] I was also rattled by an experience that happened while I was hospitalized during my second pregnancy. Many different departments at the hospital were involved in trying to solve the puzzle of my severe symptoms that turned out to be a result of the broken hardware in my spine. While I was awaiting an answer, I had an alarming interaction with the Infectious Disease Department.

October 5, 2005

A team from Infectious Disease gathered around my hospital bed this afternoon, shortly after Patrick came to see me once school was over for the day. Something about being surrounded by lab coats while I was in my flimsy hospital gown, something about them wanting to be the team that discovered what was wrong with me and how my own opinions about my body did not matter, all accumulated in a sense of powerlessness for me and put me on the defensive. None of this was helped by the conversation that then occurred.

   Infectious Disease: "Your son was born at 36 weeks. Has he had any health problems? Is this your son? (She pointed to him sitting in the chair beside my bed). He seems healthy enough."

Assumption made: How can an incompetent and disabled body like yours produce a healthy child like him?

My face burned with anger and I retorted: "What you see is what you get. He was a perfectly healthy baby and a perfectly healthy child."

Then, as soon as the words left my tongue, I was angry with myself. What, after all, is wrong or shameful if he had been "un" healthy or born with disabilities? I had, at least to a certain extent, internalized the pride and accomplishment that comes from having a healthy baby and that, very simply, pissed me off.

Although the questions were, on the surface, about the welfare of my unborn child, I strongly feel there were underlying assumptions about the health and competency of my already grown child as well as commentary about my body's abilities to create and care for these children. There exists an ideology of mother that is supposed to be someone who is able to meet all the physical, safety and emotional requirements of their babies and children.[6] Because they are not seen as being physically or sexually capable, in addition to being seen as weak, vulnerable and passive, women with disabilities are not expected to take on this social role.

Guilt

Oh, the guilt
(Nirvana, "Oh the Guilt")

Carol Gill argues that women with disabilities often feel that their medical complaints are not taken seriously by physicians.[7] Furthermore, when women with disabilities do stand up (pun intended) for their physical and medical health needs, they often feel guilty for doing so but they may also feel as though they are not being heard.[8] When advocating for a safe and accessible room or when I spoke up for my bodily needs that were related to my disability, I often felt guilty, as though I were asking for too much, or for something I did not deserve.

October 25, 2005

There is so much stress. The inaccessibility of the hospital really worries me. We have checked every single hospital room on the maternity ward and every single one won't work. The beds are too high for me to do a safe transfer; this is especially true because of my extra back problems. The toilets are all standard, and therefore too low. Although I have been offered a raised toilet seat that sits on top, I can't safely use this either because it shifts or moves. My centre of gravity is off because of my baby belly, so transfers have to be done carefully, if I can do them at all. I am already experiencing so much pain, and I am afraid of re-injuring myself like I did last week in the ante-partum ward.

We have spoken to the Patient Advocate about all of this. She was nice, but said that she doubts there can be anything done to make a room accessible when (at that time) there was a month to six weeks before the baby comes. Legally, they have to do something! I can't risk falling, especially now with my spine issues. I can't believe I have to fight this accessibility issue when I have so much else going on.

The stress continues. The inaccessibility of this room, namely the inaccessible bathroom, has been the main reason that I have gone from an independent and private person to a dependent and public person. For example, my once private matters are public now — my showers, catheterizations, bowel care, even when pads need to go underneath my behind. I feel shame and embarrassment and guilt — I need help and it isn't easy to ask for it all the time.

I still feel some of this guilt, even now. When I reflect on the source of it, I think it comes from a need to apologize for taking up too much space, needing too much extra stuff, for taking up more time, effort and money for many of the things that are effortless for non-disabled people. I think it comes from both a perception that I am somehow "getting more" than non-disabled people, like wheelchair parking or designated seating at a concert (even though the later is always a limited choice and number). I think it also comes from a need in me to apologize for wanting and yet not feeling like I deserve what other people have in their lives: love, children, gainful employment, a comfortable home, an education, some fun and the ability to get from place to place. But all of these things require adaptation, extra time, extra planning, money and compromise.

Since my second back surgery to repair my broken rods, for example, I need to drive a van with a lift instead of the small, sporty two-door car I was used to. A van is more expensive to purchase, maintain and fill with gas. It needs more space when parking to accommodate the lift. It causes more gas emissions. Another example is that one weekend this summer my niece, Tanya, and I took my children and my great nieces and nephew to a swimming pool with a waterslide. The story of how a paraplegic gets in and out of a pool with kids and a toddler is enough to write a book about, and it takes all of my grit and adaptability to make it happen. However, this complexity was lost on my (then) two-year-old, who turned to me and asked me to take her up the stairs so she could go down the waterslide. I had to tell her that I couldn't do this and that she needed to go with Patrick or an older cousin. "Okay," she sadly replied, "I need a walking person." Although I smiled at her odd use of terminology, I still felt like I was letting her down somehow. Because of these examples and countless others, I feel compelled to say, "I'm sorry" a lot — to my husband, for costing us more money, to my children, when I cannot go to the places other moms go, to the earth, for making more pollution. Disability theorist Lennard Davis echoes this: "When 'special needs' (and let us notice the valence of that term) are required, too often the person making the request is seen as overly self-concerned, overly demanding."[9] Susan Wendell also makes arguments about what I call "disability guilt" when she confesses that her "greatest psycho-ethical struggle is with guilt"[10] for not being able to do more, give more and put up with more. While I was pregnant the second time, I struggled with a lot of guilt, especially when I was hospitalized after the rods in my back broke. A large belly and broken rods made transferring extremely difficult and I grappled with the limitations of my hospital room.

October 4, 2005

I did not sleep well at all last night. My back is so sore and there are sharp pains in my ribs. Now there is a twitch in my left leg, so even though my head bobs and my eyes keep closing, I cannot fall asleep.

I tried to do my bowel routine earlier. With pads all around me I try to it in bed, which is the only safe place for me. I tried for an hour, but it just would not work. I was so frustrated. Something came over me and I felt compelled to take charge of this absurd situation. I covered myself up with a sheet, got into my wheelchair, asked the nurses to gather together the supplies I needed and I proceeded down the elevator and down the many hallways of the hospital to the bathroom on the main floor where I knew the grab bars were correctly positioned and the toilet was high and level with my chair. I realize it is bizarre and appalling to have to use a public bathroom when you are a hospitalized patient. But I felt I had few choices. I could not afford to slip, let alone fall, especially because of my back and the baby.

And I was right — the public bathroom worked. In some ways it was a metaphor for the last two weeks — my private, independent body forced to be public and dependent. I am so ashamed. And I am ashamed of being ashamed. I should be stronger than this.

When I read this now, I know that I had nothing to feel ashamed about and that it was, in fact, the hospital staff that should be ashamed that I needed to use a public bathroom while I was a patient. However, in the moment my shame and guilt were very real. It all makes sense to me now when I consider the social stigmas that are attached to being not just disabled, but also dependent, weak and vulnerable and how much, in turn, strength and independence are valued. There is also shame in asking for more than what seems deserved when one has a disability.

People with disabilities generally function at a lower social status level, and therefore asking for or demanding accommodations that bring us to the same level as everyone else can seem like we are asking for too much. I also know that by insisting on going to a public bathroom where I knew would be safer, I was taking control of my life and acting as my own advocate.

Even though he was singing about black pride and self-determination, James Brown's lyrics speak to my anger about being forced to make this decision and claiming control over my situation: "I don't want nobody to give me nothing. Open the door, I'll get it myself."[11]

Dignity

> *What it's gonna take*
> *to find dignity*
> *(Bob Dylan, "Dignity")*

Although some disability theories have given immense value to the ideas that people with disabilities should be able to live barrier-free, with access to public places and activities, as well as education and employment, the result has sometimes been a displaced emphasis on independence and a decreased emphasis on dignity.[12] It has been argued that this perspective placed too much of an emphasis on living independently and in turn created an image of people with disabilities as "the able-disabled" who are reluctant to acknowledge their weaknesses and limitations, which further perpetuates the stigma of shame that many people with disabilities endure.[13]

Cheryl Marie Wade illuminates this discrepancy between needing help and maintaining one's dignity:

> The difference between those of us who need attendants and those who don't is the difference between those who know privacy and those who don't. We rarely talk about these things, and when we do the realities are usually disguised in generic language or gimp humour. Because let's face it: we have great shame about this need. This need that only babies and the "broken" have. And because this shame is so deep, and because it is perpetrated even by our own movement when we emphasize only the able-ness of our beings, we buy into that language that lies about us and becomes part of our movement, and our movement dances over the surface of our real lives by spending all its precious energy on bus access while millions of us don't get out of bed or get by without adequate personal care. Because we don't want to say this need that shames us out loud in front of people who have no understanding of the unprivate uni-

verse we live in, even if that person is a disabled sister or brother. We don't want to say out loud a basic truth: that we have no place in our bodies (other than our imagination) that is private.[14]

October 12, 2005

I just want to go home. I don't know how I can and I know Darrell doesn't really want me there because he is so afraid of me being alone during the day and something going wrong. I don't know how I would manage anyway — having to catheterize in bed isn't hard, but it is easier psychologically without a nurse to hold the basin — it can wear at my dignity that's for sure. But bowel care — that's a tough one, I don't know what I will do about that. And although I hate this hospital bed, the way it adjusts to sitting then back to lying down is certainly advantageous when managing pain.

Frank asserts that medicine's ideals of "modernist universalism" that strives to commit equal responsibility to all persons by placing an emphasis on professional codes rather than on the specific needs of the individual patient, results in the patient's actual requirements being overlooked and undervalued.[15] This can be especially true of women with disabilities who often feel dehumanized or objectified within the medical system and who are seen solely in terms of their disabilities rather than as whole persons or complete women.[16]

October 13, 2005

Two days ago I was sent for an ultrasound of my legs to see whether or not I had any blood clots in them. When I arrived at the room, I saw the stretcher was a bit high and I was told it could not be lowered. I probably could have managed if I wasn't pregnant; however, I am just not that confident right now. My centre of gravity is off and I don't want to fall. The female technician said she would get a lift. It had harnesses for each of my legs and a hammock/sling to go around my back and that was strapped to a bar. She said that she needed a second person in the room, so she brought in a male technician. Neither of them told me their names and they worked through the process of attaching me to this lift in virtual silence. As the male technician operated the lift to start raising me up out of my wheelchair, my legs began to spread apart. Because I had been there for a leg scan, I was wearing only underwear. Even if I had been wearing pants, I would have had to take them off at that point anyway. So, with my legs spread apart, he — this guy, this total stranger — stood there, right in front of me with a complete view of my crotch. I hung there like that for at least a few minutes while the female technician tried to figure out how to operate the lift to lower me down on the table. He stared right through me. My face burned hot with shame. I could do nothing but squirm and look around for help. But no one offered to cover me, no one said a word. I was completely vulnerable, there was nothing I could do to help myself or cover or hide.

During the scan, I remembered that Cory, an athlete that I had coached in target shooting for years, and who I considered to be a dear friend, was coming to visit me later. I knew he would be able to help me back into my chair, so when the scan was finally over, I asked the technician to call down to my room to see if Cory was there, and that if he was, could he come up to the ultrasound department and help me make the transfer back into my chair so I would not have to go through this ordeal again. I knew the transfer would be easy with him. We had travelled throughout the country together, and I had relied on him for help many times, and I had never felt embarrassed for doing so. I prayed that he would receive the message.

He did. Cory hurried to the ultrasound room, and with a quick lift, I was back in my chair. When I told him what had happened with the lift and the technician, he looked at me and said, "That guy has no power over you." Through my tears, I smiled. During our coaching relationship, I had challenged Cory to mentally re-frame situations many times. When he said this to me, part of my shame dissipated, and I felt an amazing sense of reciprocity between coach and athlete.

> *I own my insecurities I try to own my destiny*
> *That I can make or break it if I choose*
> *(Sarah McLachlan, "Perfect Girl")*

This experience with the ultrasound professionals deeply affected me so much that I avoid re-reading the words of my journal entry, choosing rather to scroll down the page quickly whenever working on this chapter. When my cursor settles on Sarah McLachlan's lyrics at the end of the testimony, my heart rate slows down and I can relax, knowing that I have come to a new page.

> *Have you seen my dignity?*
> *(Bob Dylan, "Dignity")*

Invisibility

> *You don't see me but I feel so exposed*
> *(Chantal Kreviazuk, "Until We Die")*

Frank's *The Wounded Storyteller* provides some insight into why this and other incidents may have occurred while I was hospitalized. He argues that when medical professionals adhere more to the pursuit of "truth," that is, when they are more concerned with finding a diagnosis and a solution while neglecting the whole patient, they end up ignoring their responsibility to individual people. When this happens, patients' narratives end up not being understood or even heard. Certainly, as the testimonies below attest, I did not feel listened to during my pregnancies and, at times, I did not even feel as though I was seen.

November 10, 2005

In order to be induced at thirty-seven weeks, Dr. Q says Dr. L has to formally recommend it. Dr. Q says that because the baby is developing well, there are no obstetrical reasons to induce, and in doing so, we pose a risk to the baby. I asked what kind of risk and he said respiratory. I said I thought that was taken care of with the steroid shots we gave the baby a few weeks ago. This is what he led me to understand, but he responded by saying that there are no guarantees. Thirty-seven weeks is only three weeks early — it is considered full term. What about me? What about my body's health? Why can't we consider my health and how that needs to be the best it can so that I can look after the baby once she/he is born? I told him that my bladder is unmanageable, I have tremendous pain, I cannot sit for any length of time, I am compromising my back, which is already in danger. I need to be strong after the baby is here. But he won't even listen. He wants a letter. I don't think he even cares about me and my body at all. When I told him about my cough, he just smiled patronizingly and said it was an issue for my GP. He wouldn't even listen to my chest. I told him the cough was keeping me up at night and he said I could take Ativan. Ativan? I am not having panic attacks! I need to sleep.

This doctor will only be happy when I finally go away and he does not have to deal with me anymore. I only wish I had listened to myself and changed doctors a long time ago, inaccessible offices and examination tables or not.

November 16, 2005

Dr. appointment today. We saw Kristen, the resident, instead of Dr. Q which is fine with me. I feel deep resentment towards him, I don't want to see him and I don't want him to deliver my baby. He is away next week and so he has put Dr. M in charge of my care — I will meet her on Monday. And because Dr. L is fantastic to me and has recommended it, we have a date set to induce if the baby does not come on her/his own prior to that — November 28. Twelve days. I was so sure the baby would come prior to thirty-seven weeks and now I doubt it.

Gratitude

This is not my obligation
What does my body have to do
with my gratitude?
(ani difranco, "Gratitude")

A few weeks later, and just days before the date set for being induced, we received a call from a hospital staff member who was excited about the "wonderful" changes that were made to one of the hospital rooms on the post-partum ward. We were asked to come to the hospital and see the changes.

November 25, 2007

We have just toured the room that they have made accessible. They have taken a room that normally holds two people and made it for one (me). I feel uncomfortable with this vast amount of space that I do not need and will not really use. I told them it was not necessary to make a double room into a single, but of course, no one listened to that. Now I realize it probably has more to do with where the room is situated on the post-partum floor. It is in a far off corner, away from the main area. It would be absurd to put the "wheelchair room" next to the high class, expensive "Victorian room," wouldn't it?!

They have changed the toilet to a higher rise one and added a grab bar. Although a standard hospital bed is currently in the room, they assure me that a bed that raises and lowers to my chair height has been secured for use on the day that I come in to be induced. These were not huge structural changes. Why did everything have to be so stressful, negative, and complicated? Why was this situation not seen as an opportunity to make this ward friendlier? Why was I instead only seen as a complainer and a problem? It is so strange. The way they showed off the room to me sent a strong message that I am supposed to profess my undying gratitude. Yet I know I won't have much self-respect left if I do that.

November 28, 2007

I have just given birth to Chelsea a few hours ago and although I am in my "wheelchair room," I am now I am lying once again on the delivery table. The reason is simple: the bed that was supposed to be saved for me was taken by another nurse for another ward even though there was a sign on it saying not to move it. I cannot get on the bed that was in here because it is too high. Darrell was pretty upset; he asked a lot of questions and made demands that something needed to be done. This further stressed me. I just wanted to lie down. It would be okay for Darrell to help me get on the other bed but once I have to get up and say, use the bathroom, I would be stuck with the high bed again. So, because it raises and lowers to the height of my wheelchair, I opted to sleep on the delivery table. They brought it from the delivery room to my post-partum room for the night. It is quite uncomfortable — very hard on the back, but at least it lowers enough so I can transfer. I cannot believe this is happening, but honestly, I do not have the internal resources to get emotional about this. I just gave birth — I am tired.

November 29, 2005

I cannot believe what just happened. I went for a little walk with Chelsea around the post-partum ward and as I approached a group of three nurses in the hallway, I heard them talking about the room I am in. The conversation went like this:

"I cannot believe they changed the normal toilet to one of those high ones just for one patient."

"They even let her stay in a room that should hold two patients."

"Is she planning on having any more children?"

"It is amazing what some people demand."

"I hope she is grateful."

Overhearing this, I felt so shocked, so ashamed. My heart leaped up into my throat and I felt my face start to burn. Yet, I made a decision in that moment to not let them see my emotion. I wanted them to know that I had heard every word. I kept wheeling toward them. I even made eye contact. I gave them my strongest face. I would not let them get to me. And then I just kept going right on by with my new little baby girl. Screw them.

Some disability theorists, such as Susan Wendell, would argue that the above architectural inaccessibility examples are illustrations of how disability is clearly a social construction: "Disability is also socially constructed by the failure to give people the amount and kind of help they need to participate fully in all major aspects of life in the society."[17] Certainly, the absence of a room, bathroom and bed were disabling factors and authentic barriers to a safe and accommodating pregnancy, birthing and post-partum experience, but there was more to it than that. Prejudice and discrimination come in all kinds of forms. Often, it is comments like the ones of the nurses that I overheard that have the most impact. It is not as though anyone overtly de-clared that they believed I did not deserve to have children or that I did not deserve a room within which to be cared for but, nevertheless, the absence of care made strong, although unspoken, statements. Davis agrees that the worst discrimination often appears to be "trivial": "We are not speaking of people with tattoos that say, 'I hate cripples' or 'Death to Deaf!' What we are speaking of is well-meaning people who simply do not have information and education, in part because we do not teach disability in the public schools and colleges as we now teach race and gender."[18] While giving due credit to social constructionism for making great social change for people with disabilities, other disability theorists also think that the theory needs to be strengthened with the lived experiences of the body and that the vast experiences of people with disabilities is too complex to be reduced to one theory or unitary model.[19] Alexandra Howson agrees and argues that concrete examples of how the body is lived often gets written out of text and theory.[20] The medical model delegitimizes people with disabilities by defining us as abnormal, defective and less than whole. And yet, the social constructionist model, which places all the responsibility for a quality of life on the social, political and environmental aspects of society, does not take into account all aspects of the disability experience. What I am suggesting is, simply, that the experience of the body cannot be denied. The body is real, it is important and it matters. The body with disabilities has experiences that have much to offer to an understanding of all bodies. Those experiences need to be spoken. And when that happens, we just need to listen.

I am sometimes irritated with myself for not speaking up in the moment that the ultrasound technicians suspended my exposed and vulnerable body in the air. I am sometimes frustrated with myself for listening silently as the resident doctor flippantly described how the steel hardware in my back had broken. However, I take some comfort in that I am now speaking through the written word. I also take a great deal of comfort and receive much validation from Frank, who wrote about his own anger when he was ill with cancer: "When I was ill, I expressed little of this anger… because I was doing what I had to do to get by. I write now for the times I had to remain silent and for those who are still silent."[21] Similarly, I am grateful for the voice I now have.

6

Music and Joyful Embodied Experiences

For they told you life is hard …
But I'll tell you life is sweet
in spite of the misery
(Natalie Merchant, "Life Is Sweet")

Writing about my experiences is not a matter of just recording daily activities, but is rather a process of creative testimony, whereby I choose which moments get written about and how those moments will be sculpted and framed. I wrote the poem below on a day when I needed to both reflect on my losses but remain appreciative for what blessings I had. Although I do not consider myself a poet, sometimes the words I write just fall that way. On that day, the words needed to reflect on how many of my lived experiences as a pregnant woman with a disability required me to make great bodily sacrifices that were difficult and challenging, but that many of my other experiences were joyful, transformative and rewarding. Furthermore, what I am left with, namely Patrick and Chelsea, were entirely worth any sacrifices that I made.

Sacrifices:

Pain
Edema
Broken rods
Dysreflexia
Pneumonia
Broken ribs
Bone infection
Pressure sores
Weight gain
Unstable spine
Shortness of breath
Pressure sores due to edema
Racing heartbeat, even at rest
Life-threatening blood infection
Profuse sweating in reaction to pain

Lack of restorative or recuperative sleep
Permanent loss of bladder/bowel sensation
Loss of spastic activity in legs that aid in transfers and in blood circulation

Gains:

Unexpected body confidence during childbirth
Positive body experiences while breastfeeding
Two robust children who provide my life
with love, fulfillment, joy,
and meaning

Music and the Embodied Experience

I have written a great deal about the difficulties I experienced during pregnancy, but this book would be incomplete without an expression of what gifts I have received at the same time. I have tried to live my entire life with this perspective. Indeed, when I learned that the Chinese character for "crisis" communicated both danger and opportunity, I had the character tattooed on my chest. Similarly, this chapter is devoted to those sweet and happy moments I have experienced and have been forever changed by; moments that I treasure above all others.

Interestingly, these positive moments are also almost always accompanied by music. You could say I consider my life to have its own soundtrack. Sometimes music, lyrics and a pivotal life experience simultaneously correlated with my lived experience. Sometimes, the music just happened to be playing. Other times, there was a serendipitous relationship between the music "in the air" and my lived experience. Most significant to this book is how music often gives me an avenue with which to examine, re-experience, design and reframe experiences. Often called the poetry of our times, music lyrics can reverberate with people in many different ways over different contexts.

Music is often credited with creating a feeling of belonging by bringing social issues into mainstream culture.[1] Like the advent of the blues movement that was built by African-American slaves, music has a history of giving voice to oppressed or marginalized groups. A few years ago, I attended a general assembly at Patrick's school where Canadian singer-songwriter Suzie Vinnick, with her strong and passionate voice, sang and talked to the entire school population about the blues and how that music sustained the slaves escaping from the United States to Canada through the Underground Railroad. As she did this and led all the young voices to sing with her, I was moved to tears. But why? These lyrics were not written or meant for me, and yet they "spoke" to me with their expression of hope and joy as well as sorrow and despair.

Similarly, some theorists assert that while early feminism was theoretical and basically inaccessible for women who lived outside of academia, music lyrics are a way that feminist messages can become a part of social consciousness.[2] Some female music artists have stated that music is a way to illuminate women's issues by giving them voice and presence in a culture that would rather keep such issues silent.[3] To my knowledge there is no music that speaks to being pregnant or giving birth while living with a disability. Nevertheless, I was drawn to music during this time in my life and in my years as a mother probably more than I had ever been before. In a way, music made sense of and gave meaning to my lived experience. Music brought order to my chaos.

The journal entry that follows is an example of how I struggled with my new identity of being a mother when it was never expected that I would ever be a parent. Because I had internalized many societal attitudes about how people with disabilities are without sexual identities and incapable of adult social roles, I struggled with integrating the role of mother into my new life.[4] Music helped me with this integration.

Dancing to the Drum

October 7, 1996

I have spent a lot of time during this pregnancy denying that I could possibly be pregnant. Now, here I am in the hospital on my birthday and I just witnessed an ultrasound of my unborn baby. When I got back to my room from the ultrasound, the Universe continued to fit together and make sense — through music. Darrell put the CD player on, placed the headphones on my ears and played the most touching song that brought everything together and made my crazy, chaotic thinking make sense.

He had been driving home from North Battleford to Saskatoon, listening to CBC and was about to change the channel when this song came on. He knew it was just what I needed. He tried to memorize the artist's name, but the title of the song was not announced. Although he ordered that CD when he got home, when it came in, the song wasn't on it. The CD with the song was out of distribution. He didn't give up though. He went to a second hand music store, dug around, and there it was, like it was waiting for us. My reaction was more of a puzzle piece — I started crying upon hearing the first line. I wept because finally, finally, everything had come together, everything fit, it all made sense and had purpose and reason and revealed a blessed truth.

The soul of every child
has waited to be born a stranger
underneath the drum of his mother's heart
(Beth Nielsen Chapman, "Dancer to the Drum")

Dancing with Patrick

When Patrick was an infant, I, like most young mothers, was overwhelmed and not at all confident in my abilities. Since there was no ready-made script for me to follow as a wheelchair-using first-time mother, I felt I was ill-equipped to deal with this new part of my identity. I remember one time in particular. I was thinking, at three o'clock in the morning as I sat alone in the dark breast-feeding my infant son, about all the activities I would never do with him. I mourned not being able to teach him how to ride a bike or go tobogganing with him. I especially grieved not being able to have a slow dance with him, which I believed to be a special mother-son bonding, or rite-of-passage experience. In my mind, he should be tall and handsome and graduating from school or perhaps getting married, and I should be a proud mom wearing a dress with a made-for-dancing skirt with a big carnation corsage pinned just below my left shoulder. He would glide me around the floor and everyone watching would acknowledge that we were mother and son by their nods, smiles and approving looks. The more I thought about this image, the sadder I became because it felt as though that this image was not possible.

That night I descended into a depression I had not known before. Struggling with my despair, I did the only thing that seemed natural, something that I had done frequently to comfort my young self in my bedroom or hospital bed whether by a soft playing stereo or through a pair of earphones or picking up my guitar. I simply sang to him. While I did not know many children's songs, I quickly figured out that I could "lullaby" pretty much any song. As a result, the singing calmed us both and helped him to sleep. Since then, I sing to him nearly every night that we are together even though he is now eleven years old. Singing, in my "mother's voice" not only works but has transformed a coping skill into a bonding experience.

Between his second and third years, my son's appreciation for music grew beyond the need to hear the soothing and sleep-instilling sound of his mother's voice. Like me at his age, he loved to play music on the stereo. One evening, we were listening to "Elmopalooza," a recording of *Sesame Street* songs covered by popular music artists. We were dancing all over the living room and having a wonderful, laugh-filled time.

All of a sudden, a lullaby that I regularly sang to him (one of the few children's songs I knew) called "Visit the Moon" began to play. Patrick froze. He stopped his dancing and listened. He walked over to me, stepped up on the footrest of my wheelchair, looked me in the eye and said, "Mommy, this is our song. Will you dance with me?" Time, as I knew it, was paused. With tears in my eyes, I told him I'd love to. He put his arms around my waist and lay his head against my chest and we slowly danced to the entire song.

Though I would like to look down on the earth up above
I would miss all the places and people I love
And although I would like it for one afternoon
I don't want to live on the moon
(Jeff Moss, "Visit the Moon")

For me, the song illustrates how I thought I needed to have certain experiences in order to embody what it meant to be a "real" mother. I thought I wanted and needed to "live on the moon." However, while the moon might be a nice place to visit, there are many ways to experience wonder. There are many ways to know what being a mother is like.

It wasn't a special event that had brought us here. It was an ordinary day. While short in stature and in desperate need of a haircut, Patrick was undeniably handsome. We were not dressed in formal attire; we wore jeans and t-shirts. And there was no one watching. There was just the two of us, the music and the golden light of a prairie sunset pouring in through the windows, warming the room as we danced. I hope that if I am granted one memory to carry over in the moment before I some day die, it is that one.

The moment made me realize that I do not need a special occasion to mark the significance of my relationship with my son, nor do I require the approval of others in order to fully realize my role as his mother. I saw that remarkable moments are not reserved for grand events, but are available to us at any time if we choose to see them. While I learned through sport that re-framing and thereby choosing perspectives provides immense personal power, I have also learned that there is great benefit in employing these strategies in the rest of my life as well.

Chelsea Morning

The following story is about how re-framing a particular childhood memory led to an amazing series of events. I was once asked by a good friend, "If you could name your happiest childhood memory, what would it be?"

After my spinal cord was injured when I was six, I was required to spend months in hospital, an hour and a half away from my family's home on a farm. The days in the hospital were lonely; I missed my family, my school friends and my pets. With nurses looking after me instead of my mother; with hospital food served up on a tray rather than the homemade meals and farm fresh produce that I was used to; with frightening code blue calls that I would hear signaling dire emergencies in the middle of the night instead of the soothing, sleepy songs my mother would sing; and the steady invasion of needles, catheters and intravenous tubes into my little body instead of hugs, kisses and cuddles, I craved feelings of safety, familiarity and comfort.

Finally, several weeks later, I was allowed a weekend pass to go home.

My dad and brother Jim drove to the hospital to pick me up as early as was permitted for me to leave. I had not been in a car since the accident and, instead of it being a strange or scary sensation, I remember enjoying the ride, the warm breeze through the window and the sight of other people in the outside world.

When we arrived at the farm, Dad lifted me into the wheelchair and then lifted both the wheelchair and me up the steps into our house. As he raised me up the last step into our kitchen, the most beautiful sight greeted me. The sun was beaming through the window and its yellow gingham curtains made the whole room look like it was washed with gold. Mom had stayed behind to bake bread and the warm smell overwhelmed my nose and seemed to fill up my whole body. I felt welcomed home and as though it was as important to them to have me home as it was for me to feel I like I belonged there. Mom had dressed the table with the bread, farm fresh milk, jams, honey and fresh fruit. Everything was warm, sunny, joyful and as comfortable as though I had never left.

Perhaps the best part of the experience, though, was how we sat down at the table, with Dad to my left, Jim to my right and my Mom sitting directly across from me in the same configuration as we always did, how we did not talk about the accident, how we spoke only of the day and how nice it was to be together. That is what I remember best. With so many childhood memories I could have chosen, I felt compelled to pick one from a time when it seemed that I should have been the saddest. I consciously chose the memory where, although life as I had once known it would never be the same, I could still find times where I felt warm, safe and strong.

I often visit that memory in my mind whenever I need a happy thought. A handful of years after I recounted this memory to my friend, I was driving home to Saskatoon from the 1998 Rifle National Championships in Calgary. I knew the drive would be long with only myself for company, so I purchased new music for the drive. One of the CDs was Joni Mitchell's *Blue*. When "Chelsea Morning" played, I was struck by a feeling that I must have heard the song many times, but that this was my first real opportunity to listen to it. I listened to it again. Overwhelmed with memory and emotion, I began to cry. I pulled over and listened to the song over and over again.

> *Woke up, it's a Chelsea morning*
> *and the first thing that I saw*
> *was the sun through yellow curtains*
> *and a rainbow on the wall*
> *(Joni Mitchell, "Chelsea Morning")*

I felt like I had received a gift. I had already taken ownership over my perspective on my childhood by choosing my first trip home after the accident as my happiest memory. Having a song to attach to the memory gave me possession of my own history and a sense of legitimacy for my feelings and my choices.

When I arrived home I wrote down the memory and the song. I continued to reflect on and treasure the narrative that had come to feel a little like a fairy-tale. A few years later, I was marking the twenty-eighth anniversary of my car accident and, because of this event, plus many difficult issues that were occurring in my life at the time, I saw a counsellor a few times. When I told my counsellor my "Chelsea Morning" story, she sat quietly for a moment with tears in her eyes and thanked me for telling her.

The next time I saw her, she told me that she had a surprise for me. She told me about how she had been at a friend's house for dinner after she and I had our session together. She and her son had been outside playing in her friend's front yard when, shockingly, Joni Mitchell pulled up to the curb only a few houses away. My counsellor did not think twice: she walked right over to Joni and asked, "Do you have a moment?" and then, leaving out my name for confidentiality's sake, told her my story. As I listened to my counsellor tell me this, I could hardly breathe. All at once my "Chelsea Morning" story became more special, more treasured and my memory became more validated. Joni Mitchell knew my story!

Several months after that, I was reading a catalogue from our neighbourhood bookstore and while skimming the children's section, I could hardly believe my eyes when I saw a children's picture book by Joni Mitchell called *Chelsea Morning*. My hands were shaking as I held the page of the catalogue out for him to see. Darrell immediately left the house, bought the book and returned home. Holding it in my hands, I read the inside flap of the book cover that said the book was for children who see ordinary things in extraordinary ways.

A few years later, I became pregnant with my second child, a baby I "felt" quite certain was a girl. As has been detailed in previous chapters, my pregnancy became more complicated. My belly was growing and making my physical life more difficult, and whether it is a coincidence or not, the twenty-five-year-old stainless steel hardware that was keeping my spine stable succumbed to years of stress and broke, leaving me with pain, steady bouts of dysreflexia and increased difficulties with breathing, transferring in and out of my wheelchair and even just sitting.

Nevertheless, Darrell and I carried on with hope and with a focus on our little family. It was important to us to create a safe and comforting environment for Patrick. I learned this well from how my mother had made my childhood home the same way, especially on that first visit back home. I felt sure that continuing to keep our little family's life strong, optimistic, hopeful and fun was key to surviving this difficult time — after all, we would be welcoming a new baby soon. At the same time, the centennial celebration of our province was going on and a fireworks display was scheduled to occur along our city's river bank on Labour Day weekend. Patrick was desperate to go so, despite how difficult we knew it might be, Darrell and I promised him we would.

The park was full of thousands of people. We were not sure where best to watch the fireworks display but, after assessing the space, we decided to move closer to the water. Despite the amount of people, it was surprisingly dark and difficult to see where exactly we were going, but this made it all the more fun and adventurous. With Darrell pushing me and Patrick at my side, we ventured down a rough and gravelly path when suddenly the small wheels on my wheelchair hit a rut and I fell straight out of my chair, landing on my hands and knees. With the swiftness one can only really muster in a crisis like this one, Patrick held my chair while Darrell picked me up as though I weighed little more than a small child and tenderly placed me back into my wheelchair. He checked me over several times; our hearts were racing.

Just when we came to the conclusion that I seemed to be fine, we noticed that music had started playing over loud speakers set up in the park. Patrick tugged at my sleeve, then threw his arms around me, "Mom, listen, listen!" Joni's voice floated over the dark sky like a protective blanket, letting us know that all was well in the world. "Chelsea Morning" was playing.

A few months later, my baby girl was born. Darrell, Patrick and I took a good long look at her face and saw that it embodied "the sun through yellow curtains and a rainbow on the wall." I whispered in her tiny pink ear, "Pretty baby, won't you stay, we'll put on the day, and we'll talk in present tenses."

A Natural Woman

I have several journals filled with extraordinary moments that I have had with my children. One of the most significant experiences was breastfeeding. Breastfeeding both my babies were enormously satisfying and fulfilling embodied experiences that enabled me to feel great confidence in the amazing things my body could accomplish. Nursing was one of the experiences that made me feel productive, valuable and truly maternal. It was not long into my new role as Patrick's mother that I became very attached to breastfeeding, but it was not until I had given birth to Chelsea and experienced the physical trauma of the broken hardware in my back that I began to realize the reasons why nursing my baby was vital to my feelings of competency as a mother.

February 19, 2006

In thinking about it, I realize nursing makes me feel healthy and strong. When I say to myself (and I do this a lot lately), "My body is strong and healthy," I visualize breastfeeding Chelsea. This body function gives me an overall feeling of wellness, strength, productivity, and vitality. Nursing is keeping me focused in the midst of a desperate situation.

February 25, 2006

I am lying down to write this. Once again, I am having a lot of discomfort. It occurred to me that most of my body is, has become, completely unfamiliar to me: the way I look, how my clothes (don't) fit, the way the skin now hangs off my newly atrophied legs, how my bladder and bowels no longer signal any fullness, how my feet don't settle on the footrest of my chair, and of course, how obscenely crooked I am, how my left hip bone grinds against my ribs on the right side, how laborious it is to take a deep breath, how pushed up and over my intestines are, how they push food back up my esophagus causing vomit to come in my throat. And the pain. And the sweating and the unrelenting effort it takes to hold myself up all the time when I am in my chair, making it so hard to dress and change Chelsea because I have to hold myself up with my elbows on this nursing cushion that is tied around my back; and yet somehow I do this and more.

The one familiar thing about my body is breastfeeding. My breasts still work. No wonder I am so attached to it. So many people (well-meaning) continue to encourage me to give it up because they want me to have less stress. But they do not understand that I need to breastfeed so, despite everything else, I can still feel a little bit healthy, useful, female, whole, human. My cells cannot be so sick if I am nourishing Chelsea's healthy and strong cells. And sometimes I look at Patrick, doing his karate kata or practising his guitar and I think about how strong and amazing all his cells are and how I nourished them once too. It is this idea that is keeping me alive.

Therefore, although it was undoubtedly intended as a love song, it was during this time that Carole King's "(You Make Me Feel Like) A Natural Woman" became somewhat of an anthem for my embodied experience of breastfeeding and mothering. The song became part of my "self-talk."

Before the day I met you, life was so unkind
but your love was the key to my peace of mind
'cause you make me feel
like a natural woman
(Carole King, "A Natural Woman")

7

Becoming a Living Text

I'm no heroine
At least, not the last time I checked
I'm too easy to roll over
I'm too easy to wreck
(ani difranco, "I'm No Heroine")

My story is not a shining example of how to deal with adversity and I am no heroine, but I hold on to the hope that maybe someone will read my words and it will help them. The deeper I went into my writing, the more urgent the need became to share this story with others. Indeed, it felt as though my body and my life became more than just a personal story. I feel that in many ways I became a living text where there was no line between my private world and the public world for which I was writing. What I needed to share removed the need for boundaries.

Writing while Parenting

I never been laid so low
in such a meaningful way
When the mother and child reunion
is only a motion away
(Paul Simon, "Mother and Child Reunion")

Writing while parenting two young children full-time is rewarding and challenging. I wrote parts of this book between watching episodes of *Sesame Street* and playing Play-Doh with Chelsea, and between her naps and diaper changes. I put writing on hold to be with Patrick while he recovered from a tonsillectomy and ear infections and we made decisions to change schools. Many times, sewing Halloween costumes and listening to endless details about Lego projects were a greater priority than my thesis work. My office and writing space was never my own, as hard as I tried. Today, as a matter of fact, the floor is littered with crayons, puzzle pieces and Lego Bionicle parts. There is also a battery-operated toy train that mysteriously "speaks" to my wireless mouse so that every time I scroll or click, I hear "choo coo." It is funny that I have not gotten used to that yet.

Parenting and writing at the same time has proved to be more of a balancing act than I anticipated. Oftentimes I would just hit a moment of writing inspiration then look down to the clock in the corner of my computer monitor and realize I had twelve minutes to get the thoughts down because I had to dash out of the house to pick Patrick up from school (kind of like what is happening in this very moment!). Let us just say I was late a lot. I would carry a "Moleskin" notebook (and later, a pocket-book sized computer that was a Valentine's gift from Darrell) with me everywhere, so that if I had even a few minutes I could make notes. I had many inspired moments sitting in my van waiting for Patrick to finish karate class or while baking muffins, buying groceries, doing laundry or even while talking to my mom on the telephone. My body became a literal site for text because I frequently wrote on my hand. Sometimes I would write on my hand in the dark in the middle of the night and, when I woke the next morning, the damp ink would have tattooed on to my cheek if my hand rested against it while I slept.

I wrote this book on the often considered cluttered artifacts of daily living: inspired words and questions appeared on the back of grocery lists, old receipts, used envelopes and business cards; thoughts and sentences were dashed out on napkins, countless post-it notes, in Patrick's school planner and in the margins, and even on the covers, of books. Every spare moment mattered and was considered an opportunity to write. I wrote some of this book at a table in the lobby of Saskatoon's downtown movie theatre while waiting for Patrick and his friends to take in a matinee. It often felt like the needs of my children came before mine. In the end, I think that is what being a parent is supposed to be like. Perhaps my dedication to writing a little (or as it often turned out, a lot) every day and making the most out of every spare minute that I had made this book better than it would have been if I had little else but it to think about. Perhaps all those interruptions assisted the creative process that is often hard to describe. One thing I know for sure is that I do not regret a thing.

Writing while Recovering

Some are born with more and some born with less
So don't take for granted the life we've been blessed
And each one of us shall be put to the test
(Ben Harper, "The Will to Live")

Arthur Frank states: "Narratives are essential not only to the coherence of our bodies and lives. They are no less essential to the mutual recognition on which relations with others are grounded."[1] With this statement in mind, I feel it is important to make connections with people on another aspect of my life that made writing this book particularly challenging, and that is how my writing intersected with my physical and mental recovery from the two major spinal surgeries I had after Chelsea was born. The details of this experience are many and still emotionally difficult to write about. Instead of more paragraphs, making a list of the ways I was affected feels easier. A list, as opposed to a paragraph, feels more matter-of-fact and less emotional. I have also been a list-maker for years. Sometimes when there are just too many words to get out of me, making a list seems easier, simpler and like less emotional work. It has been suggested that my lists are poems, and maybe they are, but I do not call myself a poet anymore than I cannot consider myself a songwriter even though I have penned a few songs. What I do know is that sometimes a list or a poem is the way the words fall out of me and make their own form. I feel less like the creator of them and more like the vessel from which they come forth.

Recovery from:

2 spinal surgeries
6 (4 broken, 2 whole) stainless steel rods removed
8 weeks on my back, unable to angle my bed more than 30 degrees
8 weeks away from my home and family
10 litres of lost blood
10 litres of new, donated blood
20 old stainless steel screws added, then removed
20 titanium screws added
"a pinch" of active bone cells from a donor's hip joint incorporated

During my stay in the hospital I wrote a lot, but again, sometimes the words just flowed out into their own form and shape. I made this list of the "losses" I was feeling two weeks after my second surgery in October 2006. I remember the words quickly gushing out and how I felt relieved of a burden after it was finished.

During this time I lost:

My stable spine
Height
Mobility
Comfort
Pleasure
Desire
Blood

Dignity
Driving
My car
Freedom
Bathing
Showering
Power
Muscle tone
Muscle mass
Spasms (who knew I would miss them?)
Sensation
Control of my bladder
Control of my bowels
Control of my home
Control over my kitchen
Control over the food I ate
Control over the food my family ate
Independence
Strength
Motivation
Hope
Friendships
Intimacy
Privacy
Breath
Ease
Fun
Spontaneity
Simplicity
Productivity
Efficiency
Time
Quality
Imagination
Goals
Visions
Expectations
Money

Starting the writing process after so much physical and emotional trauma is a story, and a book, in itself. It was incredibly difficult and even impossible to separate what happened to my spine and the rest of my body from the experiences of my second pregnancy and childbirth. My mental state was also damaged and in need of healing. Shortly after the second surgery,

I began to write in order to begin my mental recovery and in order to start living and being productive and active again.

October 15, 2006

A List of Things I Am Not Supposed to Talk About:

I cry every day
I am hungry
I am lonely

It hurts

I am worried about getting an infection in this IV line that goes straight into my heart
I am terrified this surgery did not work
I have nightmares

I am afraid of not getting another chance

I am afraid I won't get to grow old with Darrell
I am disappointed that I have let Darrell down
I am desperately sad about all the stress I have caused Darrell, Patrick, baby Chelsea, my parents, Darrell's parents
I am super stressed about money
I am stressed about healing, or not healing

Patrick gets tired of coming to see me
Darrell is tired, irritable, impatient, and is tired of coming here too

I feel irrelevant

We cannot be confident that I am going to get rid of the infection
I do not sleep well
I don't think I have ever been so sad
Someone always has to watch me pee
Someone has to help me with a bowel movement
I have no dignity left

I am nothing

I cannot take a deep breath
I still have lots of pain
I am congested; there is no fresh air here
I have no one to talk to
I am alone

If I can't be valuable, I want to die

I have no strength left
I have no motivation
I cannot lift my baby.
There is nothing left for me.

I give up
I give up
I give up

But I did not give up. The two processes of recovery and writing fed off of each other and propelled me through the dark experiences. To recover, I had to write. To write, I had to recover.

I hope to God you haven't seen
the last part of the best of me
Oh tell me this is gonna be all right
(Serena Ryder, "Blown Like the Wind at Night")

So in order to be all right, and to find the best parts of me that I hoped still existed, I wrote for hours every day. Just as I wrote parts of this book on my hand and whatever else I could find, I also wrote down my dates, times and fasting requirements for CT scans, MRIs and bone scans on the back of journal articles that I was reading. I wrote down notes from telephone conversations with my doctor on post-it notes that ended up as bookmarks in library books. I jotted down questions I wanted to remember to ask my doctor on the blank pages of my text books while I made a career out of waiting — in hospital waiting rooms, while waiting for an x-ray or while waiting to have my blood work done. On the back of Deborah Reed-Danahay's article on autoethnography, I scrawled these thoughts to discuss with my surgeon in anticipation of his phone call to talk about my need for yet another MRI:

Is this type of test necessary? Or could I have something else? What are the alternatives?
I understand MRI needs the use of a contrast dye to show inflammation. Will the results be skewed due to my dislocated hip? Concerns: amount of radiation I am receiving and how this test will affect breastfeeding.

Writing Is an Embodied Experience

It is through these life events of parenting and recovering that I have learned that writing is an embodied experience. Writing is something I think many of us consider being cerebral, something that happens in our brains that somehow finds itself on paper or on a computer screen. In my experience, this is only part of the picture. There were many times when I would read a journal passage and when I began to transcribe it by typing on my keyboard, I would shut my eyes tight, tears springing from the corners. I would sob, howl, ache in my chest, even double over with my head resting on the desk, and still my fingers would know the words and they would type out the story. Qualitative researcher, Carolyn Ellis illustrates simply but succinctly that autoethnography is research and writing that connects the personal to the social, but that it is also "concrete action, emotion, embodiment, self-consciousness, and introspection."[2] Echoing this statement is Stacy Holman-Jones, who says that "body and voice are inseparable from mind and thought."[3] I hope to connect with readers by sharing my embodied writing process, and that my words hopefully evoke your own emotion, interest and curiosity. Perhaps, though, poet Robert Frost says it best: "No tears in the writer, no tears in the reader."[4]

I have learned that writing my personal story was not a matter of copying and pasting from my journals. Writing a story such as mine is a complex process of intense emotion, vulnerability, painful memory evocation, self-awareness, self-analysis and self-actualization. It involves reading, re-reading, writing, re-writing, analysis, rumination, more reading, more writing, more analysis and lastly, and probably most importantly, the need to be honest. It was this need to be deeply honest with myself and, therefore, with readers that I have found to be one of the most challenging parts of this writing process. By "digging deep" and revealing the "truths," I learned things about myself that I did not necessarily like and sometimes those "truths" made me uncomfortable and even ashamed. I needed to keep an open mind to the self-analysis, allowing for possibilities that I may not have otherwise considered. Through this autoethnography, I did what Deborah Reed-Danahay terms a "rewriting of the self."[5]

Also difficult for me were the comments from many of my close friends and family who had no idea what the writing process was like. Many of my family members, in particular, were clueless about what writing a thesis, or a book, entailed. When they heard "autoethnography," they tuned out to even my simplest of explanations. I heard comments even from my university-educated friends like, "If you are writing a personal story based on your journals then half your work is already done." "Writing your story must not be so hard. I mean, you have already lived it." "What is scientific about the story of one person?" The only ones who I felt truly understood and cared about me during the process were, firstly, Darrell, who saw the tear stains, the stress, frustration, confusion and fatigue printed on my very body. He also had to contend with many, many (too many) conversations about "what it all means." I could not have written this without his steady support, his wise analysis, his uncanny ability to read my mind or his brilliant ideas. Secondly, I relied on Dr. Donna Goodwin, my thesis supervisor, who I would confide in from time to time and usually right at the moment I thought I might never write another word. She inevitably had just the right words for me at those moments and I always returned to my work.

Another significant lesson I learned while writing this book is that an understanding of bodies with disabilities is essential to an understanding of all bodies. Susan Wendell argues that the experience of disability expands the variety of possible human physical experiences that the able-bodied human population may never experience.[6] The more I wrote, the more I saw that although many of the experiences I had while I was pregnant and giving birth were different than most non-disabled women experience, those different experiences need to be spoken and understood in order to provide a more complete picture of what it means to live embodied in the world. As surely as I cannot know what it is like to be an African-American little girl growing up in the deep south of the United States when I read Toni Morrison's *The Bluest Eye*, I nevertheless am a better person for having read it. I do not look like or share many of the same experiences with the main character, Pecola, but, the same time, I also connect with her "difference," her need to fit in, to be loved and to be a valuable person. I understand Pecola's desire to want to embody something neither of us ever could.

The studies of race, sexuality and gender have allowed us for some time to understand what it means to be the Other. However, with a few exceptions, disability has historically been an "added on" subject in most research and curriculum areas, not an essential core or central feature. Similarly, people with disabilities have traditionally been considered as an "added on" part of society in terms of architecture, accessibility, programs and policies and not as an integral, included part of our social fabric. An understanding of disability must include, and can only benefit from, the use of narratives, language and words in a way that have allowed us to understand race, sexuality and gender. Tonya Titchkosky reminds us that the words we use to describe people with disabilities informs our laws, practices, policies and so on and that it is these words that construe people with disabilities as outsiders and problem-causers.[7]

Sometimes people with disabilities do cause problems but, then again, so do people without disabilities. Sometimes the problem exists in the social structure; sometimes it is in the person. I am not being flippant; rather I wish to draw attention to the idea that identity, including that of disability, is dynamic and fluid, not static. Sometimes I am just a woman, sometimes a woman with a disability, sometimes a mom, sometimes a disabled mom, sometimes an athlete, sometimes a former athlete. Identity is not straightforward.[8] Foucault would add that our personalities and our identities are always changing: "Do not ask me who I am, and do not ask me to remain the same."[9] Identity is not just layered or multi-faceted or complex. It is also an action.

Universal Structures

But these stories don't mean anything
when you've got no one to tell them to
(Phillip Hanseroth, "The Story")

I have learned that this is not just the story of one person. The themes of disability, pregnancy and childbirth have the potential to resonate with others. Michel Foucault poignantly articulates: "Singular forms of experience may perfectly well harbour universal structures."[10] It is a hope that by writing my story and connecting it to the larger social world, readers will find strands of "truth" that can apply to their own lives. Empathy and connection beyond the self can contribute to meaningful sociological understandings and bring about social change.[11]

If this sounds like a call to action, it is. For far too long, I am tired of having to search through an index looking for any reference to disability. I am tired of the high shelves that do not allow me access to the best books in the library. I know I am going to need to use voice activated software some-day and that I will need a computer to handle it, and I am already worried about how much it will cost and how long it will take to learn to use. Yet, I know that people with disabilities can write the narrative of their lives if they can access to the materials to do it. They can be seen as people who have something to contribute to the social structure rather than being seen as people who need concessions. If we include people with disabilities in the planning of our social structures, the accessibility gets built in and the need for accommodations disappears. It is called universal access, and it means that everyone should have a fair opportunity to access services, buildings or products that they want and need. Universal access should be a human right.

But while the changes I have seen in the last thirty-four years are remark-able, so much more needs to be done. We need better accessibility, we need better healthcare and we need better education opportunities. For universal access to become a reality, people with disabilities need to have their per-spectives and expertise included in planning and decision-making. They first need to know that their stories matter and their voices deserve to be heard. Policy cannot be written and decisions cannot be made based solely on the story of one person, but the story of one person is where change must, and can, begin.

We also need attitudes to change. I need people to understand that it takes me a longer amount of time to do almost everything, and that just because this is so, I do not necessarily need their help. At the same time, I need it to be okay to ask for that help without embarrassment. I need to be able to take Patrick to the grocery store, ask him to carry the bags out to the car and not overhear other shoppers say how good of a "helper" and "caregiver" he is, when, in fact, he is just doing his chores. I need for people to not be shocked that Darrell actually found me attractive, and that he married me after I was paralyzed, and that those same people should not assume he is a saint for putting up with me. I need a park in our neighbourhood without gravel or sand on the ground so I can push Chelsea on the swings and catch her when she comes down the slide. I need curb cuts. I need mothers to not scoop up their children for fear that I will run over their feet because the chances of that happening are as likely as some walking person stepping on them. I need to be able to buy clothes that fit. I need doctors who are willing to admit when they do not know something about my spinal cord injury, who want to learn about what they do not know and who are open to seeing me as a whole person. I need the signs in front of designated parking stalls to say "parking for people with disabilities" or at the very least something more accurate and descriptive than "handicapped parking," which does not make any sense.

And there is more. I need people to see that autism is not a genetic problem that needs to be eliminated. I need comedians to stop making jokes about how awkward it is to be blind. I need teachers to know that attention deficit disorder really does exist and is not an excuse for being lazy. I need employers to know that in my friend, David, who is developmentally delayed, they will never find a harder and more dedicated worker. I also need David to be able to go for a walk and not be teased or harassed. I need it to be considered morally reprehensible to use the word "retard" as an insult.

I need to know that when my neighbor, Alex, discloses that he has bipolar disorder to his boss he will empathized with and not unfairly judged. My friend Jacki, who is hard of hearing, needs to be able to go to any movie she wants and have captioned access at her seat. I need my young five-year-old friend, Taylor, who has cerebral palsy, to be able to do sports, have friends, find love and live whatever life she imagines for herself. I need to see women with disabilities positively reflected in television, films, books, advertising, photographs, and yes, I dare to hope, to dream, even in music.

Who am I to say all these things? I am a just a child in a lavender gingham dress who experienced a traumatic injury that forever changed the course of her life. I am a woman who had the good fortune to be born to a fine family with extraordinarily strong and imaginative parents who helped me to fall into sport. I am an athlete that found the confidence and courage to find a life partner who has loved me for over twenty years. I am a scholar who has found a community of women with disabilities in books and music — women who gave me the courage to examine my own life and be able to then see that one person can, and does, make a difference. I am a mother whose story of pregnancy, childbirth and parenting is out of the ordinary and unusual in many ways, but who, at the same time, is really not so different from other mothers without disabilities. I am lucky enough to know that all these experiences are additive, and had they not happened I would not be writing this at all. Because of these life experiences, my time with sports and my education, I can explain it to my children. Writing this, I am counting on them to explain it to their children. And so the narrative will continue and, with that, I hold on to the faith that Sam Cooke timelessly croons, "It's been a long, a long time comin', but I know change is gonna come. Oh yes it will."

December 7, 2006

Today as I sat breastfeeding Chelsea in the waiting area before my appointment with Dr. L, my rehabilitation doctor, a young woman in her mid-twenties using a wheelchair shyly approached us.

"Is she yours?" she asked me, brushing her long brown hair from her face.

I laughed a little and assured her, that yes, this hungry little shrimp was my daughter.

Her eyes widened, and I could swear that I saw some tears spring forward. She shifted awkwardly in her wheelchair in a way that made me suspect she was still adjusting to a new cushion or a new chair. She then smiled and confessed that she had been injured for only a few months and that she was still hospitalized here at this rehabilitation unit.

"But when I leave here and go back home, I want to have a baby!" she gushed. "My husband and I have been married under a year, and although we first thought we should wait a while, we have changed our minds since the accident. Now we want to start a family soon."

Our conversation took a pause as I moved Chelsea from my right breast to my left. Although I was trying to concentrate on latching this newborn, I was aware of this woman's keen attention on what I was doing. So I offered, "If you have any questions, I would be happy to answer them. I didn't have anyone to talk with about disability stuff when I was pregnant. That would have been nice. Chelsea is just over a week old and I have a son at home who is eight."

She nodded enthusiastically and we spent the next several minutes talking about her fears that she wouldn't be able to have children, and if she were able to conceive, how she had no idea what pregnancy would be like, or if she would be able to deliver the baby without a cesarean section. She even admitted that she had wondered if breastfeeding would be possible. "Why is there so little information about women in wheelchairs who want to have kids?" she wondered out loud.

Before I was called in for my appointment, I gave her my phone number. The wide smile on her face told me she was excited about the prospect of having a child of her own. It felt good to have given her some hope.

Epilogue

Now that you've grown up
You can finally learn to be a child
(Ben Harper, "Skin Thin")

I am holding my book. It is still warm off the printer. At some point I have to be satisfied. The athlete in me is not dead, and because of that I will always believe that there is more work to do and more improvements to be made. And yet, I know I must let it go. When I was little, I wrote in diaries to keep myself company when I was lonely. Now I write because I have to let the stories out, and because I want to share them. By sharing them, I bring voice to what has been unspoken. This deeply matters to me; I feel it is my life's purpose.

June 4, 2008

It is the 32nd anniversary of my car accident. I always mark the day in some special way. This year Patrick, Darrell and I celebrated by going to see k.d. lang in concert. While writing this book, I have realized that there are few lines between my academic or public life and my private life during the writing of this autoethnography, not even, as it turns out, when attending a spectacular concert on the most personal of days. But when I heard k.d. sing "Coming Home," I reached into my purse to find a piece of paper, any piece of paper, and a pen, any writing utensil would do. And in the dark I scrawled that inspired and meaningful line, "I am happily indifferent to the ones who have consistently been wrong."

I do not know if I am always happily indifferent to the ones who have consistently been wrong about me, but I do know that I strive to be. Some days I get it right. Other days I struggle. The autoethnographic process has made me realize that I am living an extraordinary life and that I have a body worth celebrating. My body has done, and continues to do, incredible things. The lack of expectations that surrounded me as a woman with a disability were not ones I had to necessarily live with. I am an agent. It is hard work. But it is good work.

I secretly wish that through some miracle of time travel or an alternate universe, this book could magically land in the hands of my six-year-old self,

131

her parents, her teachers and her doctors. I wish I could let them know that it was all going to turn out okay, that everything works out, and even better than they might have hoped. Since that is not possible, I wish for the next best thing: I wish that this book lands in the hands of someone else who needs it, maybe another little girl, or maybe a young woman who wants to be a mother.

Notes

Notes for Chapter 1

1. Foucault, *The history of sexuality: An introduction*.
2. Butler, *Gender trouble*.
3. Fine and Asch. *Women with disabilities: Essays in psychology, culture, and politics*; Garland-Thomson, "Extraordinary bodies"; Mairs, "Carnal acts"; Wendell, *The rejected body: Feminist philosophical reflections on disability*.
4. Fine and Asch, *Women with disabilities*; Garland-Thomson, "Integrating disability, transforming feminist theory"; Gill, "The last sisters: Disabled women's health."
5. Gabel and Peters, "Presage of a paradigm shift? Beyond the social model of disability toward resistance theories of disability"; Olkin, *What psychotherapists should know about disability*.
6. Gabel and Peters.
7. Olkin, p. 110.
8. Olkin; Wendell.
9. Foucault.
10. Garland-Thomson, "Integrating disability, transforming feminist theory," p. 22.
11. Gill, "Four types of integration in disability identity development."
12. Gill, p. 42.
13. Gill, p. 43.
14. Merleau-Ponty, *Phenomenology of perception*.
15. Merleau-Ponty.
16. Garland-Thomson, "Integrating disability, transforming feminist theory," p. 18.
17. Grue and Laerum, "'Doing motherhood': Some experiences of mothers with physical disabilities."
18. Finger, *Past due: A story of disability, pregnancy, and birth*; Grue and Laerum.
19. Longhurst, "Corporeographics of pregnancy: 'Bikini Babes,'" p. 453.
20. Howson, *Embodying Gender*.
21. Diprose, "Corporeal generosity: On giving with Nietzsche, Merleau-Ponty, and Levinas."
22. Thomas, "The baby and the bath water: Disabled women and motherhood in social context."
23. Lipson and Rogers, *Pregnancy, birth, and disability: Women's healthcare experiences*.
24. Garland-Thomson, "Integrating disability, transforming feminist theory."
25. Garland-Thomson.
26. Garland-Thomson.
27. Mullin.
28. Mullin, p. 45.

Notes for Chapter 2

1. Weiss and Haber, *Perspectives on embodiment: The intersections of nature and culture*; Wendell, *The rejected body: Feminist philosophical reflections on disability.*
2. Mullin, *Reconceiving pregnancy and childcare.*
3. Chouinard, "Body politics: Disabled women's activism in Canada and beyond," "Connecting our lives with yours: Why disability is every woman's issue"; Fine and Asch, *Women with Disabilities: Essays in Psychology, Culture, and Politics*; Gill, "The last sisters: Disabled women's health"; Wendell.
4. Titchkosky, *Reading and writing disability differently: The textured life of embodiment*, p. 8.
5. Wendell.
6. Gill.
7. Wendell, p. 93.
8. Bredahl, "Participation of people with disabilities in adapted physical activity research"; Peters, "Disablement observed, addressed, and experienced: Integrating subjective experience into disablement models"; Titchkosky.
9. Garland-Thomson, "Integrating disability, transforming feminist theory."
10. Reed-Danahay, *Auto/ethnography.*
11. Wendell.
12. Wendell.
13. Berube, "Foreword: Side shows and back bends," p. x.
14. Titchkosky, p. 12.
15. Garland-Thomson, p. 6.
16. Muncey, "Doing autoethnography," p. 7.
17. Wendell.
18. Ellis, *The ethnographic I: A methodological novel about teaching and doing autoethnography.*
19. Sparkes, "Autoethnography: Self-indulgence or something more?"
20. Sparkes, "The fatal flaw: A narrative of the fragile body-self."
21. Sparkes, p. 467
22. Holman-Jones, "Autoethnography: Making the personal political," p. 765.
23. van Manen, *Researching lived experience: Human science for an action sensitive pedagogy*, p. 73.
24. Ettore, "Gender, older female bodies and autoethnography: Finding my feminist voice by telling my illness story."
25. Greig, "Female identity and the woman songwriter."
26. Greig.
27. Pople, *Theory, analysis, and meaning in music.*

Notes for Chapter 3

1. Lorde, *Breast cancer journals: Special edition*, p. 59.
2. Frank, *The wounded storyteller: Body, illness, and ethics.*
3. Frank, p. 18.
4. Frank, p. 25.
5. Krassioukov, Furlan and Fehlings, "Autonomic dysreflexia in acute spinal cord

injury: An unrecognized clinical entity."

6. Diprose, *Corporeal generosity: On giving with Nietzsche, Merleau-Ponty, and Levinas.*
7. Howson, *Embodying gender.*
8. Garland-Thomson, "Integrating disability, transforming feminist theory"; Foucault, *The archaeology of knowledge*, p. 135.
9. Tremain, *Foucault and the government of disability.*
10. Butler, *Gender trouble.*
11. Garland-Thomson, p. 16.
12. Wendell, *The rejected body: Feminist philosophical reflections on disability*, p. 81–82.
13. Wendell, p. 81.
14. Garland-Thomson; Wendell.
15. Wendell, p. 84.
16. Mullin, *Reconceiving pregnancy and childcare.*
17. Chouinard, "Connecting our lives with yours: Why disability is every woman's issue," "Body politics: Disabled women's activism in Canada and beyond"; Fine and Asch, *Women with disabilities: Essays in psychology, culture, and politics*; Gill, "The last sisters: Disabled women's health"; Mullin; Thomas, "The baby and the bath water: Disabled women and motherhood in social context"; Wendell.
18. Asch, 2001; Fine and Asch; Grue and Laerum, "'Doing motherhood': Some experiences of mothers with physical disabilities"; Mullin; Neville-Jan, "Selling your soul to the devil: An autoethnography of pain, pleasure and the quest for a child"; Prilleltensky, "My child is not my career: Mothers with physical disabilities and the well-being of children," "A ramp to motherhood: The experiences of mothers with physical disabilities."
19. Grue and Laerum; Prilleltensky, "My child is not my career," "A ramp to motherhood."
20. Kuttai, "Dancing with disability and mothering: Examining identity and expectations."
21. Gill, "The last sisters: Disabled women's health," p. 101.
22. Fine and Asch, p. 21.
23. Gill, "Four types of integration in disability identity development."
24. Gill, "The last sisters: Disabled women's health."
25. Verduyn, "A deadly combination: Induction of labor with Oxytocin/Pitocin in spinal cord injured women, T6 and above."
26. Gill, ""The last sisters: Disabled women's health."
27. Gill, "The last sisters: Disabled women's health"; Lipson and Rogers, *Pregnancy, birth, and disability: Women's healthcare experiences*; Mullin.
28. Mullin.
29. Shakespeare, "Joking a part."
30. de Beauvoir, *The second sex.*
31. Wendell, p. 60.
32. Wendell, p. 88–89.
33. de Beauvoir.
34. Holland et al., "The power and degradation of female sexuality."
35. Young, *Justice and the politics of difference.*
36. Mullin.
37. Mullin, p. 45.

38. Mullin; Young, 1984
39. Fine and Asch; Gill, "The last sisters: Disabled women's health"; Wendell.
40. Thomas.
41. Zitselsberger, "(In)visibility: Accounts of embodiment of women with physical disabilities and differences, p. 394.
42. Lorde, p. 19.
43. Garland-Thomson.
44. Garland-Thomson.

Notes for Chapter 4

1. Garland-Thomson, "Integrating disability, transforming feminist theory," p. 7.
2. Jenkins, *Sport science handbook: The essential guide to kinesiology, sport, and exercise science* 2.
3. Orlick, *Psyching for sport: Mental training for athletes* and *In pursuit of excellence: How to win in sport and life through mental training*.
4. Jenkins, p. 171.
5. Lynch and Huang, *Working out working within*.
6. Reed-Danahay, *Auto/Ethnography*, p. 4.
7. Garland-Thomson.
8. Frank, *The wounded storyteller: Body, illness, and ethics*, p. xii.
9. Frank, p. 3.
10. Parsons, *The social system*.
11. Frank, p. 6.
12. Frank.

Notes for Chapter 5

1. Wendell, *The rejected body: Feminist philosophical reflections on disability*, p. 39.
2. Wendell, p. 39.
3. Gill, "The last sisters: Disabled women's health."
4. Morris, "Impairment and disability: Constructing an ethics of care that promotes human rights."
5. Morris, p. 4.
6. Mullin, *Reconceiving pregnancy and childcare*.
7. Gill.
8. Wendell.
9. Davis, *Bending over backwards: Disability, dismodernism and other difficult positions*, p. 125.
10. Wendell, p. 4.
11. Brown, "I don't want."
12. Wendell.
13. Wade, "It ain't exactly sexy."
14. Wade, p. 89.
15. Frank, *The wounded storyteller: Body, illness, and ethics*.
16. Gill, "The last sisters: Disabled women's health."
17. Wendell, p. 40.

18. Davis, p. 137.
19. Corker and Shakespeare, *Disability/Postmodernity: Embodying disability theory*; Shakespeare and Watson, "The social model of disability: An outdated ideology?"
20. Howson, *Embodying gender.*
21. Frank, *At the will of the body: Reflections on illness*, p. 114.

Notes for Chapter 6

1. Whiteley, *Sexing the groove: Popular music and gender.*
2. Paglia, *Sex, art, and american culture: Essays.*
3. Kaplan, "The politics of feminism, postmodernism, and rock: Revisited, with reference to Parmar's righteous babes."
4. Fine and Asch, *Women with disabilities: Essays in psychology, culture, and politics.*

Notes for Chapter 7

1. Frank, "For a sociology of the body: An analytical review," p. 89.
2. Ellis, *The ethnographic I: A methodological novel about teaching and doing autoethnography*, p. xix.
3. Holman-Jones, "Autoethnography: Making the personal political," p. 767.
4. Frost, "The figure a poem makes," p. ii.
5. Reed-Danahay, *Auto/Ethnography*, p. 4.
6. Wendell, *The rejected body: Feminist philosophical reflections on disability.*
7. Titchkosky, *Reading and writing disability differently: The textured life of embodiment.*
8. Shakespeare and Watson, "The social model of disability: An outdated ideology?"
9. Foucault, *The archaeology of knowledge*, p. 17.
10. Foucault, *The history of sexuality: An introduction*, p. 335.
11. Sparkes, "Autoethnography: Self-indulgence or something more?"

References

Berube, M. (2002). Foreword: Side shows and back bends. In L. Davis (ed.), *Bending over backwards: Disability, dismodernism and other difficult positions* (pp. vii–xii). New York: New York University Press.

Blume, J. (1970). *Are you there God, it's me, Margaret*. New York: Dell Publishing.

Bredahl, A. M. (2007). Participation of people with disabilities in adapted physical activity research. *Sobama Journal, 12*, 74–79.

Butler, J. (2006). *Gender trouble*. New York: Routledge.

Chouinard, V. (1999). Body politics: Disabled women's activism in Canada and beyond. In R. Butler and H. Parr (eds.), *Mind and body spaces: Geographies of illness, impairment and disability* (pp.269–94). London: Routledge.

Chouinard, V. (2005). Connecting our lives with yours: Why disability is every woman's issue. In L. Biggs and P. Downe (eds.), *Gendered intersections: An introduction to women and gender studies* (pp. 344–48). Halifax, NS: Fernwood.

Corker, M., and Shakespeare, T. *Disability/postmodernity: Embodying disability theory*. New York: Continuum.

Davis, L. (2002). *Bending over backwards: Disability, dismodernism and other difficult positions*. New York: New York University Press.

de Beauvoir, S. (1952). *The second sex*. New York: Alfred A. Knopf.

Didion, J. (1966). On keeping a notebook. In *Slouching towards Bethlehem* (1969). London: Andre Deutch.

Diprose, R. (2002). *Corporeal generosity: On giving with Nietzsche, Merleau-Ponty, and Levinas*. London: SUNY.

Duncan, M. (2004). Autoethnography: Critical appreciation of an emerging art. *International Journal of Qualitative Methods, 3*, 1–14.

Ellis, C. (2004). *The ethnographic I: A methodological novel about teaching and doing autoethnography*. Walnut Creek, CA: Alta Mira.

Ettore, E. (2005). Gender, older female bodies and autoethnography: Finding my feminist voice by telling my illness story. *Women's International Forum, 28*, 535–46.

Fine, M., and Asch, A. (eds.). (1988). *Women with disabilities: Essays in psychology, culture, and politics*. Philadelphia, PA: Temple University Press.

Finger, A. (1990). *Past due: A story of disability, pregnancy, and birth*. Seattle, WA: The Seal Press.

Foucault, M. (1984). *The history of sexuality: An introduction*. Toronto: Random House.

Foucault, M. (1969). *The archaeology of knowledge*. New York: Pantheon.

Frank, A. (2002). *At the will of the body: Reflections on illness*. New York: Houghton Mifflin Company.

Frank, A. (1995). *The wounded storyteller: Body, illness, and ethics*. Chicago: The University of Chicago Press.

Frank, A. (1993). *The diary of a young girl.* New York: Bantam.

Frank, A. (1991). For a sociology of the body: An analytical review. In M. Featherstone, M. Hepworth, and B. Turner (eds.), *The body: Social processes and cultural theory* (pp.36-102). London: Sage Publications.

Frost, R. (1939). The figure a poem makes. *Collected Poems of Robert Frost.* New York: Holt, Rinehard, and Winston.

Gabel, S., and Peters, S. (2004). Presage of a paradigm shift? Beyond the social model of disability toward resistance theories of disability. *Disability and Society, 19,* 585–600.

Garland-Thomson, R. (2002). Integrating disability, transforming feminist theory. *National Women's Studies Association Journal, 14,* 1–32.

Garland-Thomson, R. (1997). *Extraordinary bodies. Figuring physical disability in American culture and literature.* New York: Columbia University Press.

Gill, C.J. (1997a). The last sisters: Disabled women's health. In S.B. Ruzek, V. Olesen, and A. Clarke (eds.), *Women's health: Complexities and differences.* Columbus, OH: Ohio State University Press.

Gill, C. J. (1997b). Four types of integration in disability identity development. *Journal of Vocational Rehabilitation, 9,* 39–46.

Greig, C. (1997). Female identity and the woman songwriter. In S. Whitley (ed.), *Sexing the groove: Popular music and gender* (pp.168–77). New York: Routledge.

Grue, L., and Lerum, K.T. (2002). 'Doing motherhood': Some experiences of mothers with physical disabilities. *Disability and Society, 17,* 671–83.

Holland J., et al. (1994). The power and degradation of female sexuality. *Feminist Review, 46:* 21–39.

Holman-Jones, S. (2005). Autoethnography: Making the personal political. In N. K. Denzin and Y. S. Lincoln (eds.), *The handbook of qualitative research* (3rd ed., pp. 763–92). Thousand Oaks, CA: Sage.

Howson, A. (ed.), (2005). *Embodying gender.* London: Sage.

Iovine, V. (1995). *The girlfriend's guide to pregnancy: Or everything your doctor won't tell you.* New York: Pocket Books.

Jenkins, S. (2005). *Sport science handbook: The essential guide to kinesiology, sport, and exercise science, 2.* Essex, UK: Multi-Science Publishing.

Kaplan, E. A. (2002) The politics of feminism, postmodernism, and rock: Revisited, with reference to Parmar's righteous babes. In J. Lochhead and J. Auer (eds.), *Postmodern music postmodern thought* (pp. 323–34). New York: Routledge.

Kuttai, H. (2005). Dancing with disability and mothering: Examining identity and expectations. In L. Biggs and P. Downe (eds.), *Gendered Intersections: An introduction to women and gender studies* (pp. 254–58). Halifax, NS: Fernwood.

Krassioukov, A.V., Furlan, J.C., and Fehlings, M.G. (2003). Autonomic dysreflexia in acute spinal cord injury: An unrecognized clinical entity. *Journal of Neurotrauma, 20,* 707–16.

Lipson, J., and Rogers, J. (2000). Pregnancy, birth, and disability: Women's healthcare experiences. *Healthcare for Women International, 21,* 11–26.

Longhurst, R. (2000). Corporeographics of pregnancy: 'Bikini babes.' *Society and Space, 18,* 453–72.

Lorde, A. (1997). *Breast cancer journals: Special edition.* San Francisco, CA: Aunt Lute.

Lynch, J., and Huang, C. (1998). *Working out working within*. New York: Penguin Putnam.

Mairs, N. (1986). *On being a cripple*. Plaintext. Tuscon: University of Arizona Press.

Mairs, N. (1996). Carnal acts. In P. Foster (ed.), *Minding the body: Women writers on body and soul* (pp. 267–82). New York: Doubleday.

Merleau-Ponty, M. (1962). *Phenomenology of perception*. New York: Routledge.

Morris, J. (2001). Impairment and disability: Constructing an ethics of care that promotes human rights, *Hypatia, 16*, 1–16.

Morrison, T. (1970). *The bluest eye*. New York: Plume.

Mullin, A. (2005). *Reconceiving pregnancy and childcare*. Toronto: Cambridge University Press.

Muncey, T. (2005). Doing autoethnography. *International Journal of Qualitative Methods, 4*, 1–11.

Murkoff, H., Eisenberg, A., and Hathaway, S. (2002). *What to expect when you're expecting*. New York: Workman Publishing Company.

Neville-Jan, A. (2004). Selling your soul to the devil: An autoethnography of pain, pleasure and the quest for a child. *Disability and Society, 19*, 113–27.

Olkin, R. (1990). *What psychotherapists should know about disability*. New York: Guilford Press.

Orlick, T. (1986). *Psyching for sport: Mental training for athletes*. Champaign, IL: Leisure Press.

Orlick, T. (2000). *In pursuit of excellence: How to win in sport and life through mental training* (3rd ed.). Windsor, ON: Human Kinetics.

Paglia, C. (1990). *Sex, art, and American culture: Essays*. New York: Vintage.

Parsons, T. (1951). *The social system*. New York: Free Press.

Peters, D. J. (1996). Disablement observed, addressed, and experienced: Integrating subjective experience into disablement models. *Disability and Rehabilitation, 18*, 593–603.

Pople, A. (1994). *Theory, analysis, and meaning in music*. Toronto: Cambridge University Press.

Prillentensky, O. (2003). A ramp to motherhood: The experiences of mothers with physical disabilities. *Sexuality and Disability, 13*, 21–47.

Prillentensky, O. (2004). My child is not my career: Mothers with physical disabilities and the well-being of children. *Disability and Society, 19*, 209–23.

Reed-Danahay, D. (1997). *Auto/Ethnography*. New York: Berg.

Shakespeare, T. (1999). Joking a part. *Body and Society, 5*, 47–52.

Shakespeare, T., and Watson, N. (2002). The social model of disability: An outdated ideology? *Research in Social Science and Disability, 2*, 9-28.

Sparkes, A. (2002). Autoethnography: Self-indulgence or something more? In A. Bochner and C. Ellis (eds.), *Ethnographically speaking: Autoetnography, literature, and aesthetics* (pp. 209–32). New York: AltaMira.

Sparkes, A. (1996). The fatal flaw: A narrative of the fragile body-self. *Qualitative Inquiry, 2*, 463–94.

Titchkosky, T. (2007). *Reading and writing disability differently: The textured life of embodiment*. Toronto: University of Toronto Press.

Thomas, C. (2007). The baby and the bath water: Disabled women and motherhood in social context. In A. O'Reilly (ed.), *Maternal theory: Essential readings* (pp.

500–19). Toronto: Demeter Press.

Tremain, S. (2005). *Foucault and the government of disability.* Ann Arbor, MI: The University of Michigan Press.

van Manen, M. (1990). *Researching lived experience: Human science for an action sensitive pedagogy.* London, ON: The Althouse Press.

Verduyn, W. (1994). A deadly combination: Induction of labor with Oxytocin/Pitocin in spinal cord injured women, T6 and above. Unpublished manuscript. Presented at the Conference on the Health of Women with Disabilities, National Institutes of Health, Bethesda, MD.

Wade, C. M. (1994). It ain't exactly sexy. In B. Shaw (ed.), *The ragged edge: The disability experience from the pages of the first fifteen years of The Disability Rag* (pp. 88–90). Louisville, KY: Advacado Press.

Weiss, G., and Haber, H.F. (1999). *Perspectives on embodiment: The intersections of nature and culture.* New York: Routledge.

Wendell, S. (1996). *The rejected body: Feminist philosophical reflections on disability.* New York: Routledge.

Whiteley, S. (1997). Introduction. In S. Whiteley (ed.), *Sexing the groove: Popular music and gender.* New York: Routledge.

Young, M. (1990). *Justice and the politics of difference.* Toronto: Cambridge University Press.

Zitselsberger, H. (2007). (In)visibility: accounts of embodiment of women with physical disabilities and differences. *Disability and Society, 20,* 389–403.

Music

Jann Arden. (1995). Good mother. Living under june. Fontana: A and M Records.

Bad Religion. (2000). Don't sell me short. The new America. Atlantic Records.

James Brown. (1969). I don't want. Say it loud: I'm black and proud. King Records.

Beth Nielsen Chapman. (1993). Dancer to the drum. You hold the key. Reprise.

Edwyn Collins. (1994). Low expectations. Other songs. Bar/None Records.

Sam Cooke. (1964). Change is gonna come. Ain't that good news. RCA Victor.

ani difranco. (1992). Fixing her hair. Imperfectly. Righteous Babe Records.

ani difranco. (1992). I'm no heroine. Imperfectly. Righteous Babe Records.

ani difranco. (1994). Overlap. Out of range. Righteous Babe Records.

ani difranco. (1994). Gratitude. Like I said. Righteous Babe Records.

Dire Straights. (1985). Why worry. Brothers in arms. Warner Brothers.

Bob Dylan. (1994). Dignity. The best of Bob Dylan, Vol. 3. Columbia Records.

Phil Hanseroth. (2007). The story. The story. Sony Music Canada.

Ben Harper. (1997). The will to live. The will to live. EMI Virgin Music.

Ben Harper and Relentless 7. (2009). Skin thin. White lies for dark times. Virgin Records America, Inc.

Indigo Girls. (1992). Virginia woolf. Rites of Passage. Sony Records.

Etta James. (1961). At last. At last. Universal Music Group.

Carole King. (1971). (You make me feel like) A natural woman. Tapestry. Ryko Distribution.

Chantal Kreviazuk. (1999). Until we die. Colour moving and still. Columbia

Records.

Eileen Laverty. (2006). The Road. Ground beneath my feet. B.R.C Music Canada.

Annie Lennox. (2007). Lost. Songs of mass destruction. Sony Music.

Gordon Lightfoot. (2002). Beautiful. Complete greatest hits. Rhino/WEA.

Sarah McLachlan. (2004). Perfect girl. Afterglow. Arista.

Natalie Merchant. (2005). These are days. VH1 Storytellers [DVD]. Warner Bros.

Natalie Merchant. (1998). Life is sweet. Ophelia. Elektra.

Joni Mitchell. (1971). Chelsea morning. Blue. Reprise Records.

Jeff Moss. (1978). I don't want to live on to the moon. Elmopalooza. Sony Music.

Nirvana. (1993). Oh the guilt. Puss/Oh, the guilt. Tough and Go Records.

Our Lady Peace. (2002). Story about a girl. Gravity. Sony Music Entertainment Canada.

Xavier Rudd. (2007). Better people. White moth. Xavier Rudd/Salt X Records.

Serena Ryder. (2009). Blown like the wind at night. Is it o.k. [CD]. Atlantic Records.

Shad. (2008). Brother (Watching). Old prince. Black Box Canada.

Paul Simon. (1988). Mother and child reunion. Negotiations and love songs 1971–1986. Warner Bros.

Nina Simone. (1989). Don't let me be misunderstood. Don't let me be misunderstood. Island Def Jam.

Tegan and Sara. (2009). Hell. Sainthood. Sire/Wea.

The Au Pairs. (2006). Stepping out of line. Stepping out of line: The anthology. Sanctuary/Castle.

Stan Vincent. (1970). Ooh child. [Recorded by the Five Stairsteps]. Greatest Hits. Buddah Records.

Stevie Wonder. (1976). Sir duke. Songs in the key of life. Motown Record Company.

Neil Young. (2003). Stayin' power. Hawks and doves. Reprise Records.

Neil Young. (2009). When worlds collide. Fork in the road. Reprise Records.